Praise for *Scrum Shortcuts without Cutting Corners*

"Great books give you advice you can follow, and *Scrum Shortcuts without Cutting Corners* most definitely does. Written to suit newcomers or experienced practitioners who have a healthy interest in Scrum, the knowledge contained in this book can be game-changing. Ilan Goldstein shares his extensive global experience to produce a well-written and valuable insight into practicing and sustaining effective agile practices."

—Kevin Austin, Agile coach and transition lead, Fortune 50 investment bank

"A software team succeeds because it has the right people who are allowed to do their best work. Understanding the patterns and anti-patterns (my favorite anti-pattern—'test sprint') in this guidebook will help you know who the right people are and how to help them work well. These shortcuts focus on people, and that's why they work. Get your team (and the rest of your company) reading and discussing this today."

—Lisa Crispin, coauthor with Janet Gregory, of *Agile Testing: A Practical Guide for Testers and Agile Teams*

"Ilan Goldstein has earned a loyal following in the Agile community for his no-nonsense advice and practical solutions that deliver real results for teams. I'm thrilled that he's been able to distill this expertise into a book that's rich with insights and also very readable. I can't wait to use all his best ideas in my own practice!"

—Pete Deemer, CEO of Stormglass and author of *The Scrum Primer*

"This book is an outstanding reference for anyone using Scrum to build software. Whether you are an experienced practitioner or a beginner just starting out, you'll find something worthy in here that you can learn and apply right away. Ilan's casual and engaging writing style describes perfectly the real-world challenges that you may face when using Scrum, and gives you practical guidance for working through them."

—Ryan Dorrell, CTO, AgileThought

"I especially like the essay style. It invites me to skip around to find topics of interest, and makes it easy to find what Ilan thinks about things. Ilan takes us over ground we've covered before, but he gives us a fresh look at things. Very valuable!"

—Ron Jeffries, coauthor of *The Agile Manifesto* and founder of xpr━━━━━━ .com

"Scrum is not a solution. Your solution _____ ourney of inspection and adaptation. The journey _____ vill make some mistakes as you try to customize S_____ work for me is a Hitch Hiker's Guide to Scrum, g_____ ches, and belief to support you. I really appreciate t_____ Ilan's stories and how he shares his experiences. I don't have to agree with every technique or idea, as Ilan is not trying to instruct. He is asking you to think; to challenge your assumptions and help you on your way."

—Martin Kearns, Scrum trainer and national Agile and innovation lead at
  SMS Management & Technology

"Most books about Scrum are on theory and speak from a distant third-person perspective. They are hard to read. Ilan has created the opposite. He has created a book that feels like a conversation. I kept nodding in recognition at all the real-world problems he identifies and laughing at the pragmatic, humorous, and spot-on wisdom he shares. His writing flows smoothly and draws you in to the point where you will hate to put this book down at the end."

—Clinton Keith, Scrum trainer and author of *Agile Game Development with Scrum*

"With *Scrum Shortcuts without Cutting Corners*, Ilan Goldstein has delivered the must-have text for Scrum teams. The fact that Scrum is a framework is often used to justify tinkering with its fundamental mechanisms—to the extent that what was once Scrum becomes something altogether different and less effective. Goldstein clearly identifies the delineation between those mechanisms that can be tailored and those that must remain true to ensure success."

—Arik Kogan, business intelligence manager at Cougar Software

"A refreshing perspective on Scrum. Ilan will take you beyond the theory and share his real-world experiences, offering practical advice for successful Scrum adoption and maturity within your organization. His insights and philosophical views on the subject will keep you one move ahead in the game."

—John Madden, program manager at HotelsCombined

"Ilan has done some great work here. This book is an insightful look at what it takes to grow as a Scrum Master, and provides practical real-world experience to guide you on the journey. It's part practical advice and part story-telling woven together to make a book that is useful and enjoyable to read at the same time. I enjoyed the book and look forward to having a copy on my bookshelf. Ilan has done a wonderful job."

—Kane Mar, Scrum trainer; cofounder and president of Scrumology.com

"Scrum is deceptively simple, but as someone said, it is easy to do this in a mediocre way. I have fallen into many of the traps myself. In his book, Ilan shows you how to succeed with Scrum. The book makes it easy to find the information that is most helpful to you right now. Each of the many short chapters is to the point and a pleasure to read. I couldn't recommend it more."

—Jens Meydam, head of development, Zahnärztekasse AG

"Ilan's book isn't the usual cookbook on how to use Scrum in the workplace, but rather a toolkit of practical advice that covers every aspect of setting up self-organizing, high-performing teams using Scrum. It is a highly engaging, enjoyable and meaningful read for all Scrum practitioners."

—Michael Rembach, applications development manager, Transport for New South Wales

"Ilan's valuable tactics, tools, and tips for applying Scrum clearly illustrate his own hard-fought, on-the-job experience. This is not a theoretical book about Scrum, but instead a practitioner-focused, get-your-hands-dirty guide to getting the job done with Scrum. It is a delightful read with topics presented concisely and in an easily digestible way. *Scrum Shortcuts without Cutting Corners* is a critical addition to the body of Scrum literature, and a perfect follow-on to my *Essential Scrum* book!"

—Kenny Rubin, managing principal, Innolution, LLC and author of *Essential Scrum: A Practical Guide to the Most Popular Agile Process*

"If Scrum and Agile were easy, everybody would be doing it! Now that so many are, this book is the virtual Agile coach I wish I had when I was on the early steps of my Scrum journey. Ilan is a world-class coach, and he has packed this book full of ideas and approaches to all of the common questions and issues that are bound to come up as you transform your world of work to Scrum."

—Craig Smith, Agile coach and editor at InfoQ

"If *The Scrum Guide* is the rule book, then *Scrum Shortcuts without Cutting Corners* is the experts' guide to playing the game. Ilan Goldstein reveals all the little secrets that every team should know to be effective in adopting Scrum. From sprint lengths, to splitting down work, to relative estimation, Ilan tackles the gray zones in Scrum, offering sage advice in a world of 'it depends.'"

—Renee Troughton, Agile coach and author of *Agile Forest*

"Sharing what he has learned implementing Scrum over many years with many teams, Ilan goes beneath the surface and gives practical tips to help you raise your Scrum teams to the next level. With humor, trivia, and stories from personal experience, *Scrum Shortcuts without Cutting Corners* is an accessible and adaptable Scrum recipe book ScrumMasters can use in any environment. Whether you have a few months or many years of experience with Scrum, this book will give you new ideas on how to approach whatever challenges are facing your team."

—Liza Wood, ScrumMaster and blogger at *Sockets and Lightbulbs*

SCRUM SHORTCUTS WITHOUT CUTTING CORNERS

Scrum Shortcuts without Cutting Corners

Agile Tactics, Tools, & Tips

Ilan Goldstein

✦Addison-Wesley

Upper Saddle River, NJ • Boston • Indianapolis • San Francisco
New York • Toronto • Montreal • London • Munich • Paris • Madrid
Capetown • Sydney • Tokyo • Singapore • Mexico City

The publisher offers excellent discounts on this book when ordered in quantity for bulk purchases or special sales, which may include electronic versions and/or custom covers and content particular to your business, training goals, marketing focus, and branding interests. For more information, please contact:

U.S. Corporate and Government Sales
(800) 382-3419
corpsales@pearsontechgroup.com

For sales outside the United States, please contact:

International Sales
international@pearsoned.com

Visit us on the Web: informit.com/aw

Library of Congress Cataloging-in-Publication Data
Goldstein, Ilan.
    Scrum shortcuts without cutting corners : agile tactics, tools & tips / Ilan Goldstein.
        pages cm
    Includes bibliographical references and index.
    ISBN 978-0-321-82236-9 (paperback : alkaline paper)
  1. Agile software development—Handbooks, manuals, etc. 2. Scrum (Computer software development)--Handbooks, manuals, etc. I. Title.
    QA76.76.D47G645 2013
    005.1—dc23   2013016569

ISBN-13: 978-0-321-82236-9
ISBN-10:   0-321-82236-6
Text printed in the United States on recycled paper at RR Donnelley in Crawfordsville, Indiana.
Second printing, September 2014

*To my little Amy, the cutest impediment one could ever hope for,
and to my soul mate Carmen, the greatest ScrumMaster of all!*

CONTENTS

FOREWORD

In the spirit of this book, I'll take a shortcut and come right to the point: Buy this book. I assure you, you'll find the wisdom in this collection of shortcuts extremely helpful.

However, experience tells us to be leery of shortcuts. Very few work out. Horror movies begin when a group of teenagers take a shortcut through the woods on a dark night. The driver on a family trip opts for what looks like a shortcut and is reminded for years about how it turned out not to be. We're told "there are no shortcuts to success," and that success comes from a combination of perseverance and skill.

Yes, in life many shortcuts do not work out. The shortcuts in this book are different. They work.

I first met Ilan Goldstein online when a web search led me to his blog of Scrum shortcuts. He hadn't written many shortcuts by then, but the few he had were tremendously helpful—and funny. Ilan's sense of humor shone through in every shortcut.

It didn't take a genius to see that Ilan was onto something with his shortcuts. And so I asked him if he'd consider writing a book of shortcuts. This book is the result. In it, Ilan offers thirty tips, covering the full gamut of a Scrum implementation. He offers tips on getting started, on requirements, on estimating and planning. There are tips about quality and metrics, about team members and roles, about managing bosses, and about continuous improvement. If you've struggled with it on a Scrum project, it's likely Ilan has a shortcut to help you.

Ilan has been there and done that. His tips come from his experience as a Scrum-Master and Certified Scrum Trainer. His shortcuts all come from routes he's traveled. They're practical, not theoretical. Further, I like that he's not afraid to take a stand. Too many books rely too often on the consultant's standard answer of, "It depends." You won't find that here.

Whether you are a month, a year, or a decade into Scrum, you will find shortcuts here that will help you improve. I wish you well on your Scrum journey. I know you'll arrive more quickly by following the shortcuts in this book.

—Mike Cohn
   Co-founder of the Scrum Alliance and the Agile Alliance
   Author of *Succeeding with Agile*

PREFACE

"Ah, so it's the opposite of Dilbert" was my psychiatrist friend's reply when I gave him the quick overview of Scrum. (And no, I wasn't seeing him to deal with the stress of writing my first book while my first baby kept me up all night!) Anyway, after a chuckle, I realized that not only had my friend distilled Scrum so simply and elegantly, but also, I had just found my opening quote!

Scrum and its agile cousins comprise the next serious evolution in vocational process and culture. I'm certainly not alone in observing that this is possibly the greatest leap forward since the advent of scientific management, aka Taylorism. (By the way, did you know that a certain Henry Gantt of painful stripy-chart fame was a disciple of Taylor?) Scrum throws away the dictatorial, power-is-cool, ego-driven management approach that views people as replaceable cogs in a defined-process machine. Instead, Scrum treats teams as groups of responsible, dedicated free-thinkers who, given the opportunity, will work in an optimal fashion to derive the most positive outcome.

It is tremendously exciting and a privilege to be in the vanguard of this change together with our early Scrum pioneers who are still energetically leading the charge. No doubt in decades to come, this period in time will be recognized as an era when a significant shift occurred in the way the workplace operates.

Why Did I Write This Book?

I recall a conversation that I had with Martin Kearns, another Australian-based Scrum trainer, who pointed out to me that like it or not, people are going to read this book (with its assortment of tactics, tools, and tips) and consider it to be an official user manual—something that they should follow to the letter. This highlighted a concern that I was already feeling: how could I offer specific, focused advice that cuts through the theory and straight to the chase without making it seem too prescriptive? The answer to that question is to explain that *Scrum Shortcuts without Cutting Corners* is about sharing with you *an* approach rather than *the* approach to implementing Scrum. How can you have more than one approach to Scrum? you might be wondering. This question is explained clearly by Kenneth Rubin in his book, *Essential Scrum* (2012):

> Scrum is based on a small set of core values, principles, and practices (collectively the Scrum framework). Organizations using Scrum should embrace the

Scrum framework in its entirety; however, this doesn't mean that each organization's Scrum implementation will be the same. Rather, each organization will have its own unique implementation of the Scrum framework based on the specific approaches that it chooses to realize the Scrum practices. . . . An approach is a particular implementation of a Scrum practice.

There are many other approaches, with their own sets of tactics, tools, and tips that you can and should explore, but I hope that the ones that I lay out in this book will, at the very least, trigger some thought and offer you some tried and tested options.

I wrote this book because, along my journey, I have acquired a significant number of cuts and bruises from tripping over stumbling blocks and banging my head against brick walls—frankly, implementing Scrum is really tough! It makes a whole lot of sense when the theory is explained to you, but gee whiz, try to get it up and running effectively and it is anything but trivial. Over a number of years, and after working with several teams, I finally began to see some return on investment from the bodily harm that had been inflicted. I had created an adaptable (and emergent) Scrum recipe book that worked across numerous different teams and several organizations, and I realized my hard-earned knowledge could help out others working in similar environments.

Back to my chat with Martin, as he also offered me some helpful advice: noting that I had just become a new parent for the first time, he asked me whether I thought I should try to protect little Amy from every situation in which she might fall and hurt herself. My heart said, "Absolutely, I won't let anything hurt my little girl," but my brain realized that you have to let even those you care about trip over (on occasion) to learn what works and what doesn't. That being said, though, you certainly always want to be there to comfort them and to give them some helpful advice for next time. So, this book is just that—the helpful advice for "next time" to start limiting the extent of your cuts and bruises moving forward. I'm assuming that you have at least given Scrum a shot, so you are likely already carrying some old wounds, but with any luck, this book will protect you somewhat from the next round of knocks.

If, however, you are new to Scrum and really hate cuts and bruises, feel free to jump right in. Perhaps some of this advice will keep you injury-free . . . for a while. But bear this in mind: every project is different, every team is different, and every organization is different. So if you're expecting to successfully apply every piece of advice on every page, then I would like to realign your expectations right now before you are disappointed—honestly, there is no magic approach that will work across the board.

Finally, for those of you who feel you've pretty much got this whole Scrum thing all worked out and under control, I hope that by browsing this book you are able to find some interesting new tools to add to your Scrum toolbox.

Some Assumptions

Most of the lessons that I share throughout this book were obtained while I was a hands-on ScrumMaster in several organizations, and as such, the book's primary audience is the ScrumMaster. However, that certainly doesn't exclude others from benefiting, including product owners, developers, and senior stakeholders. Even my attorney wife, without an ounce of interest in the software scene, found it useful and interesting—so there you go!

I also assume that you are not brand new to Scrum. I expect that you have read a few books, perhaps attended some entry-level training, and even tried working with Scrum for a period of time. If you fall into this camp, this book is intended to help you reach the next level of Scrum efficiency and maturity by expanding and extending your Scrum toolbox.

If you are brand new to Scrum, never fear: this book contains many chapters (or *shortcuts*) that you will still be able to easily relate to. However, I recommend that you at least read one or all of the following short Scrum overviews:

- *Core Scrum* (Scrum Alliance, 2012)
- *The Scrum Guide* (Schwaber and Sutherland, 2011)
- *The Scrum Primer* (Deemer, Benefield, Larman, and Vodde 2010)

For a more comprehensive introduction to Scrum, I highly recommend you pick up Rubin's recently published book, *Essential Scrum* (Rubin 2012).

How to Use This Book

I didn't write this book sequentially, so don't feel obliged to read it in that manner. Although the book is broken up into logical sections, you can easily jump around to your heart's content without losing continuity.

The shortcuts are written to be quickly and easily absorbed. My goal is to ensure that they are so easy to digest that even in the heat of battle, they can come to your aid. Alternatively, during peaceful times, they can act as some useful yet entertaining reading while you wait in line for the office microwave at lunchtime.

Speaking of lunchtime, you can treat *Scrum Shortcuts without Cutting Corners* like a recipe book (or a spell book if you just so happen to be a wizard or witch)—simply flip to the shortcut you're after, decide whether the ingredients work for you, and if not, feel free to add your own spices . . . at your own risk. With any luck, out of the oven will materialize an immediately useful and highly practical approach to tackling a particular Scrum challenge.

My Goals

This book is not just about helping make Scrum work for you. It is also meant to help you elevate your Scrum teams to the next level of effectiveness and maturity. Most of what I've written is not covered in any Scrum guide (nor even in your typical Scrum-Master training course). Instead, these are real-world approaches to the Scrum practices that have been properly tested under fire.

A point worth reiterating is that I don't expect you to follow what is written in this book to the absolute letter. However, I do recommend that during your constant quest for continuous improvement, you at least experiment by inspecting a selection of these tactics, tools, and tips and adapting your own processes to see whether they lead to improvements. Ideally, you not only will benefit from my approach but will be able to further evolve it and teach me a thing or two!

ACKNOWLEDGMENTS

I can humbly admit that I completely under-estimated the efforts required to turn my nebulous thoughts into the published work that you're reading right now. Looking back now, I still can't believe how it all eventually came together! Writing a book requires extreme focus, follow-through, and open-mindedness but most importantly it requires help. This help comes in many shapes and forms and without it, there would be no book. There are many people who went above and beyond to help make this book what it is today and I am extremely grateful to each and every one of them who gave me a hand along the way.

Let's start from the very beginning of the journey so that I can firstly thank my main man, Colin Tan—business partner, art designer, in-the-trenches proofreader and best pal. He was the one who prodded me in the first place to start sharing my Scrum-thoughts with the world and without him you wouldn't be reading this book—simple as that. I'm sure that you'll agree that his artwork adds a unique, creative dimension to this book that the words alone cannot deliver.

I would next like to deeply thank Superman, aka Mike Cohn. I call him Superman for a couple of reasons. Now, everyone knows how much of a huge positive impact Mike has made on the Scrum world through his seminal books and community involvement, but not many of you know that he is also a power-lifting champion who can bench-press 560 pounds! I kid you not. Superpowers aside, being invited to write a book for Mike's series is a career high-watermark that is going to be ridiculously hard to top.

To Chris Guzikowski, Olivia Basegio, and Chris Zahn at Pearson, who helped me traverse the unfamiliar world of publishing and who patiently answered all of my questions throughout the process—I thank you for everything. Also, I'd like to thank Carol Lallier and Elizabeth Ryan who did such a great job pulling everything together at the end.

I'd like to thank the other Signature Series authors: Lyssa Adkins, Jurgen Appelo, Lisa Crispin, Janet Gregory, Clinton Keith, Roman Pichler, and Kenny Rubin not only for welcoming me into the team but also for providing me with inspiration long before I started writing this book. I'd especially like to thank Kenny Rubin for all of the valuable tips that he was able to offer me, having completed his own fantastic book, *Essential Scrum*, at the same time that I started writing this one.

Now to the reviewers: I will always be thankful for the time you took out of your busy lives to share your opinions and offer your thoughts. First I'd like to thank Cecil Goldstein, aka Dad: I bet you thought that your homework-proofing days were long over, but nevertheless, you happily came out of retirement, and your feedback was as valuable as ever.

I would also like to extend my gratitude to the following people who offered such helpful feedback throughout the long journey: Kevin Austin, Joel Bancroft-Connors, Jeremie Benazra, Charles Bradley, Mario Cueva, Pete Deemer, Ryan Dorrell, Caroline Gordon, Doug Jacobs, Ron Jeffries, Martin Kearns, Joy Kelsey, Richard Kaupins, Arik Kogan, Venkatesh Krishnamurthy, John Madden, Kane Mar, Jens Meydam, Nicholas Muldoon, Bryan O'Donovan, Michael Rembach, Matt Roadnight, Peter Saddington, Lisa Shoop, Craig Smith, Hubert Smits, Michael Stange, Renee Troughton, and Jason Yip.

To the Scrum and broader agile community, I thank you collectively for maintaining such an amazing culture of openness and for always being so willing to share ideas. I truly hope that this book will further contribute to the hugely positive influence that this community has already made in transforming the world of work.

Finally, to my amazing wife, Carmen, who did everything possible to give me every spare Pomodoro of time to write in the throes of all sorts of chaos, including precariously navigating through our first round of parenthood! You really are a Scrummy Mummy! And to little Amy, for allowing me just enough sleep to write at least semi-coherently, but mostly, for just being the most amazing inspiration and making everything worthwhile.

ABOUT THE AUTHOR

Ilan Goldstein is an avid agilist with over a decade of practical hands-on experience. He is a globally recognized Certified Scrum Trainer (CST) working with start-ups, market leaders, government agencies, and public companies around the world, helping them to improve their agility through the implementation of Scrum. He is a regular conference speaker, guest university lecturer, and founder of both AxisAgile—a leading provider of agile training and consulting services—and Scrum Australia—a national not-for-profit organization focused on growing and enriching the Scrum community Down Under.

Ilan is a dedicated Scrum practitioner, relishing the time that he has spent as a ScrumMaster, developer, and product owner (not at the same time of course!) on a number of projects within a variety of environments and industries. He is acutely aware of what it takes to transform theory into practice and this knowledge is shared both within this book and the Scrum training that he conducts around the world.

Ilan holds a number of professional certifications that augment the war wounds that he has accumulated achieving his numerous in-the-trenches Scrum victories. These include: Certified Scrum Trainer (CST), Certified Scrum Professional (CSP), Certified ScrumMaster (CSM), Certified Scrum Product Owner (CSPO), Project Management Professional (PMP), as well as Agile Certified Practitioner (PMI-ACP).

He lives in Sydney, Australia, with his wife Carmen and daughter Amy and in his spare time volunteers for Compeer, the award-winning, global mental health program.

For more information, visit www.axisagile.com. Ilan can also be found on Twitter as @ilagile and can be contacted via e-mail at ilan@axisagile.com.

Chapter 1

SCRUM STARTUP

Taking that first step on any unfamiliar journey can be daunting and fraught with challenges. Questions such as *Where do we start?*, *How do we start?*, and most important, *Why should we start?* can often turn into momentum-dampeners that impact an organization's goal of adopting a new framework such as Scrum.

The following three shortcuts aim to help you and your organization answer these tough questions and to put some spring into that first step!

Shortcut 1: Scrum on the Pitch provides guidance to assist in "selling" Scrum to those in your organization involved in its adoption. Shortcut 2: Fragile Agile identifies a selection of common pitfalls to watch out for during the early days of your Scrum journey. Finally, Shortcut 3: Creative Comfort discusses a range of steps to ensure an environment and culture that fosters a healthy Scrum team.

Shortcut 1: Scrum on the Pitch

Scrum is seriously not a tough sell. I must admit that obtaining buy-in for Scrum these days is almost like shooting fish in a barrel. Okay, well, maybe it's not quite that easy, although I don't think anyone would disagree with the observation of Ken Schwaber, cocreator of Scrum, that "Scrum appears to have crossed the chasm and is now more mainstream than radical" (Schwaber 2011). This progress has certainly made the lives of the new generation of Scrum evangelists somewhat easier than it was for our pioneers. At the very least, it means that we no longer have to withstand as many strange stares when we start presenting software development using descriptions borrowed from the sport of rugby!

On that note, let's first tackle the question you've no doubt been asked many times in your Scrum-promoting travels: "What does SCRUM stand for?" Many people (even so-called qualified ScrumMasters) use this capitalized spelling, implying that Scrum is an acronym. If you fall into this camp, you might be surprised when I tell you that Scrum is *not* an acronym and was actually named after rugby's scrum (yes, all lowercase this time).

For those not familiar with the sporting variety of scrum, it is a tight pack of burly, 250-ish-pound rugby players linked together like a jigsaw puzzle who work as one to drive back their opposition while progressing down the pitch (field) toward their try-line (scoring zone). It is this concept of tight, self-organizing, collaborative teamwork that gave birth to the agile development version of the word. This initial comparison was described by Takeuchi and Nonaka (popularly known as

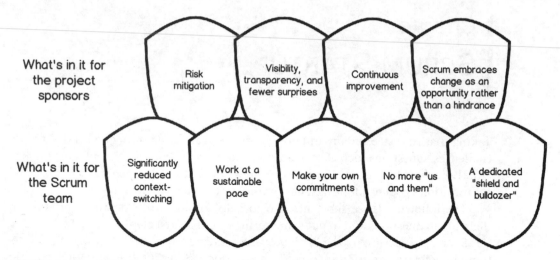

FIGURE 1.1   Just like a Spartan phalanx—impenetrable if discipline is maintained.

the godfathers of Scrum) in their groundbreaking paper, "The New New Product Development Game" (Takeuchi and Nonaka 1986). Hailing from a rugby-passionate country, I have witnessed the sporting scrum in action. It is similar in concept to the ancient Spartan shield-locking phalanx (see Figure 1.1)—immensely powerful if discipline is maintained and teammates work together as one.

Werewolf Slayers?

Convincing stakeholders of the efficacy of Scrum is a job that I just love to do! Why? Well, I get a buzz seeing eyes light up when I talk about transparency, early delivery of business value, reduced waste, and risk mitigation. Further, it excites me when I hear the sigh of relief when I put forward the drastic notion that change should no longer be viewed as a hindrance but as an opportunity.

All that being said, we Scrum enthusiasts unfortunately are not werewolf slayers with a pack of silver bullets. The reality is that while the concepts behind Scrum are simple and intuitive, implementing them successfully is anything but simple.

So, what is it about Scrum that has made it the most popular agile framework? The answer to that question depends on who you are pitching to—the Scrum team (including the ScrumMaster, product owner, and developers) or the senior stakeholders (let's call them the project sponsors). The rest of this shortcut focuses on the trigger points that most appeal to these two key groups.

Let's start with a great quote from Mike Cohn, one of the founders of both the Scrum Alliance and the Agile Alliance, which makes for a great initial elevator pitch:

> Scrum is an agile framework that allows us to focus on delivering the highest business value in the shortest time. (Cohn 2007a)

Okay, sounds good so far! Now, let's get more specific and start explaining to our two groups what's in it for them.

The Scrum Team

Let's begin by exploring some key benefits that we can promote to the Scrum team, consisting of the ScrumMaster, product owner, and developers.

Reduced Context-Switching

The all-too-common tap on the shoulder with yet another request to work on something "more urgent" is removed. Scrum provides the construct of the *protected sprint* (which I personally like to call "fixed flex"). The protected sprint allows the developers to completely fix their focus on what they committed to during the sprint planning session (see Shortcut 8) while also offering the product owner flexibility to modify the broader product backlog throughout the project.

Sustainable Pace

I'm not going to lie and say that if you adopt Scrum there will never be any late nights. That being said, Scrum is all about working at a steady, sustainable pace to avoid those last-minute, mistake-laden cram sessions. Scrum decimates the traditional culture of heroically working late nights and weekends just to prove how dedicated one is to the cause.

Rubin (2012) makes the point nicely:

> One of Scrum's guiding principles is that team members must work at a sustainable pace. (No more death marches!) In doing so, they deliver world-class products and maintain a healthy and fun environment.

No More Delegating Dictators

No longer does the dictatorial, delegation-addicted project manager determine who's doing what and when it needs to be done by. Instead, the establishment of self-organizing teams is one of Scrum's flagship goals. These empowered teams determine how the work will be tackled because they are the ones actually doing the work!

No More "Us and Them"

Although Scrum respects and appreciates an individual's uniqueness, the idea of personal achievement is overshadowed by team achievement. Gone is the specific performance monitoring of individuals, not to mention any us-and-them mentality between various development functions. With Scrum, everyone pitches in to the maximum extent that they can to help the team finish what it collectively committed to completing.

A Dedicated "Shield and Bulldozer"

Nothing is more abhorrent to a focused developer than having to deal with politics, interruptions, and impediments. Thanks to the servant-leader ScrumMaster role (see Shortcut 4), the development team can focus on what it does best—developing great software. The ScrumMaster protects the team from disruptive outside influences and removes issues that may be impeding development progress.

Hopefully, you now have the future team convinced and ready to give Scrum a go.

Project Sponsors

Next, let's uncover a selection of key benefits that pertain to our higher-level project sponsors.

Risk Mitigation

If you think about it, on a traditional software project, there is 100 percent risk and 0 percent business value delivered until the final day of the project when the software is (hopefully) released successfully. Massive 18-month release cycles incorporating waterfalling phases don't offer meaningful insight or value until right at the very end (see Figure 1.2).

By delivering working, quality functionality incrementally, the Scrum team provides genuine business value to the customer in weeks (or days) rather than months (or even years), and the risks are significantly reduced thanks to the faster feedback cycles.

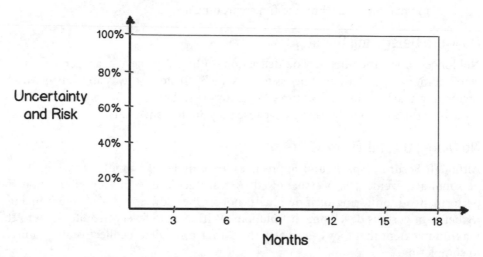

FIGURE 1.2   Waterfall projects carry 100 percent risk until the end of the project.

Visibility, Transparency, and Fewer Surprises

Visibility is particularly pertinent for organizations whose project sponsors don't have a software development background. To these sponsors, development can often appear to be a very opaque black box offering zero visibility. Scrum, however, is grounded in empirical process control that promotes transparency as a core tenet. It is achieved in part via easy-to-understand "information radiators" (such as the task board—see Shortcut 21) as well as regular sprint reviews that everyone is invited to.

Continuous Improvement

Along with transparency, the other two pillars of empirical process control are inspection and adaptation. These important elements are applied to both the product under development and the development process being utilized to ensure that continuous improvement is occurring across the board. "Inspect and adapt" is Scrum's core mantra.

Change Is an Opportunity

No longer do product sponsors have to ruffle feathers when they come up with a great new idea that they want to add to the product backlog mid-project. Referring back to the concept of fixed flex, the project sponsors, with the permission of (and via) the product owner, are liberated and welcome to add to the product backlog as they see fit, at any stage throughout the project.

Good News and Not-So-Good News

See, I told you it was easy! The good news is that I don't think you'll find many members in either of the key groups who won't get at least a little bit excited by what Scrum has to offer.

The not-so-good news, though, is that however easy it might be to sell Scrum, backing up your pitch with a highly effective Scrum implementation is a very different story. Even for those of you who may have managed to get a Scrum implementation off the ground, getting your team humming like a finely tuned Scrum Ferrari rather than a beat-up old Scrum Pinto requires patience, an open mind, and some scrapes and bruises along the way, as well as handy books like this one!

Shortcut 2: Fragile Agile

Possibly one of the most frustrating comments that I hear when speaking to novice software teams is, "We do Scrum—we work in sprints, we have a daily scrum, and we even have a product backlog." In addition, although they may not explicitly say it, you can often add, "We don't write any documentation, we release haphazardly, we plan on the fly, and we don't care about buggy code because we'll just fix it up with a bug iteration." *ARGH!* These people give Scrum a terrible name, and worse still, when their projects inevitably fail, it is very difficult, if not impossible, to win back the senior stakeholders who have been burnt by a badly warped Scrum implementation.

It's a Framework, Not a Method

You will often hear Scrum described as a method—this description is incorrect. Scrum is a framework of practices tied together by a small set of clearly defined rules. There are significant differences between a method and a framework. A method implies a one-size-fits-all, formulaic approach, whereas a framework offers a more flexible platform from which a variety of approaches can be derived depending on the environment.

To correctly implement Scrum, it is important to follow the few prescribed rules and to work within the framework of practices. So long as the approaches you choose to implement adhere to this premise, you are on the right track. As Schwaber (2011) writes in his blog, "Scrum is like chess. You either play it as its rules state, or you don't." Extending this analogy, we can say that implementing the Scrum framework partially is like choosing to play chess with 20 pieces instead of the standard 32 pieces. Although there is a slim chance that the game will work in some form, the fact is that the 20-piece adaptation is an alternative and untested game that shouldn't be called chess (see Figure 1.3).

Scrum does not contain redundant rules or practices. As such, for it to work as intended, it must be implemented holistically—partially adopting Scrum is tantamount to not adopting it at all.

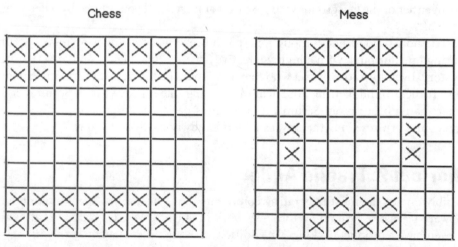

FIGURE 1.3   Just as you wouldn't change the rules of chess, you shouldn't change the rules of Scrum.

Qualifications versus Qualities

A ScrumMaster certification is certainly helpful, but depending on who is getting certified, it still might not mean all that much. I recall years ago, during my first ScrumMaster course, one attendee was a project manager from a bank who seemed to believe he was the drill sergeant from the movie *Full Metal Jacket*.[1] I remember thinking to myself that even if this course went for 2 years, this guy would never get it. The bottom line is that the qualities of a ScrumMaster (see Shortcut 4) are significantly more meaningful than a certification.

Abusing the Agile Manifesto

Those who tend to warp Scrum may even occasionally quote the words of the Agile Manifesto (Beck et al. 2001) to justify their complete lack of documentation and absent planning:

Manifesto for Agile Software Development

We are uncovering better ways of developing software by doing it and helping others do it. Through this work we have come to value:

- **Individuals and interactions** over processes and tools
- **Working software** over comprehensive documentation
- **Customer collaboration** over contract negotiation
- **Responding to change** over following a plan

That is, while there is value in the items on the right, we value the items on the left more.

Anyone who abuses the Agile Manifesto in such a manner has either (a) not read the final line, (b) forgotten the final line, or (c) ignored the final line.

It is extremely important to remember that while the items on the left are valued more, the items on the right are almost always needed even if they are required in only a limited capacity (depending on the type of project).

A Few Scrum Antipatterns

What follows is a sample selection of symptoms that will immediately indicate that Scrum is being corrupted and warped. These symptoms should not be confused with "teething" issues faced by novice (yet genuine) Scrum teams. For example, a daily scrum that doesn't always start on time is not ideal, but with the right motivation, it is a process that can improve and isn't necessarily a signal that the team simply doesn't get it.

---

1. www.imdb.com/title/tt0093058.

Test Sprints

Quality assurance should be treated as an integral part of the development process. A requirement should not be considered done unless it has met the quality requirements stipulated in the definition of done (see Shortcut 11). However, sometimes the message gets twisted. When this happens, it tends to manifest as an initial bunch of "functionality" sprints that focus purely on banging out new code (to give the impression that progress is happening), followed by a bunch of "catch-up" sprints for identifying and fixing bugs.

The typical justification for this behavior is that the team wants to validate their work by at least showing the general functionality to the users of the software first. When I come across this situation, I point out to the team that just because they might be working in sprints, it doesn't mean that they aren't waterfalling. Remember that until the functionality is fully tested and releasable, it is not complete and should be considered unreleasable (therefore useless) and very high risk.

Another implementation of this antipattern is the scenario in which the programmers and testers are working in different sprints: for example, the testers may be working one sprint behind. This situation arises primarily when automated testing practices are still immature and reliance on manual regression testing is still heavy. This staggered sprint scenario inevitably leads to the same catch-up sprints just discussed.

Never-Ending Sprint Zeros

Sprint zero isn't really a sprint but an artificial term often used to describe the preliminary work that a team might undertake before it is ready to commence an actual sprint (with all of the required trimmings).

This preliminary work doesn't typically have a timeframe, nor does it exhibit all of the typical structural elements found in a real sprint, such as a sprint backlog and well-formed requirements.

Although I'm not a fan of the misleading sprint zero label, I don't actually have an issue with the concept of a preliminary stage. My main problem with sprint zero arises when inappropriate work is bundled into it that delays the starting of real sprints. Let's take a look at what should and what shouldn't go into any sprint zero (see Figure 1.4).

Just because the items in the Don't Include list in Figure 1.4 might appear more nebulous than the concrete functional requirements, it doesn't mean they can't be estimated, planned, and broken down into tasks and therefore included in a sprint. In fact, I would argue that because of the nebulous nature of this work, it is even more important to wrap the proper sprint mechanics around it in order to offer greater visibility and tighter control.

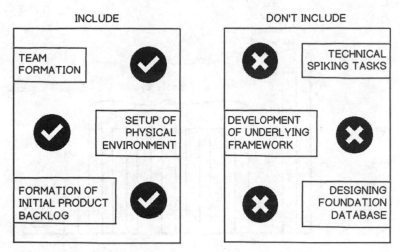

FIGURE 1.4   Sprint 0 tasks should be kept to the bare minimum.

Random-Sized Sprints

A regular sprint duration is important for a number of reasons that are outlined in Shortcut 8.

One of the most common excuses I hear for sprint length fluctuation is that the team wanted to sneak in a few extra days to finish some *nearly* complete requirements so that the sprint review is more compelling.

I believe there are only two reasons for varying the sprint length:

- When a new team is experimenting in the early days following initial formation.

- When all work is completed before the last day of the final sprint (see Figure 1.5).

Estimation Isolation

This situation has been prevalent in every non-Scrum environment I've worked in. It is instigated when a senior developer is asked in isolation to estimate the duration of various pieces of work. You might well ask why this is a problem considering that someone so senior should be the most qualified to offer estimates. Well, this is exactly one of the problems. Although the senior developer might be the most experienced, in most cases he or she won't be doing the actual work. The senior developer's abilities will no doubt differ from the abilities of the team members who actually tackle the tasks, and so it follows that his or her estimate is going to differ from the eventual reality.

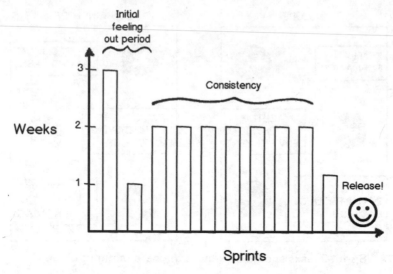

FIGURE 1.5   Once determined, maintain a consistent sprint duration.

In addition, it isn't an individual who is doing the work—it is the team—and as such the team as a collective should make the estimation (see Shortcut 14). When only one person conducts the estimation, there are no checks and balances in place. What if the individual is having an off day or perhaps misheard some vital detail and made an incorrect assumption? When a group of diverse team members is involved, such slips are much less likely to occur thanks to the multiple layers and filters processing the information.

Reliance on the Spec

If you start hearing comments such as "If it's not in the spec, it won't get done" or "I implemented exactly what was in the spec," you can also be sure that your clothes are already wet courtesy of the waterfall that the team is standing in. It also demonstrates that your team members have become bureaucrats who have lost their ability to communicate with other human beings. Any so-called spec should exist only as a placeholder or reminder, and the actual requirements will manifest in both the dulcet tones coming out of the team's collective voice box as well as in the actual working software that the team produces.

Poor ScrumMaster Selection

If your ScrumMaster doesn't maintain the attributes detailed in Shortcut 4 and/or doesn't perform the functions detailed in Shortcut 26, then you are more than likely being led by an imposter. How do you spot an imposter? Well, if the ScrumMaster is making unilateral product or technical decisions, micromanaging task assignments, driving the team to put in regular overtime, or generally acting like a tyrant, then there are going to be problems.

Listen to Your Folks

Heed the advice that your parents probably gave you once or twice: If you're going to do something, do it properly. In the same way that you wouldn't change the parameters of chess, you shouldn't change the parameters of Scrum. Either implement Scrum within the boundaries of its framework or don't call what you're doing Scrum.

Shortcut 3: Creative Comfort

Does this sound familiar?

> *ScrumMaster:* "Good morning guys!"
>
> *Developer 1:* (Grunts)
>
> *Developer 2:* (Barely recognizable nod)
>
> *Developer 3:* (Headphones on and no facial recognition detected)

Once upon a time, this typical morning ritual was one of the most annoying aspects of coming to work. The morning greeting, the most trivial of human interactions, would always put me in an irritable mood to kick start the day. Why? Simply because interactions similar to the one described can make you feel as though you're entering a shrine rather than a hive of productivity.

Some of you might think it's somewhat lame to cheerily say good morning on a particularly cold and gray Monday morning: "We're engineers, damn it, not bubbly sales people," I hear some of you say. Tell me something: If you went over to your pal's home, would you mumble a greeting under your breath and sit on the couch without saying anything further? I doubt it, but if you did, how do you think your pal would feel? Pretty annoyed, I would imagine.

A smile and a genuine "How are you?" makes you feel that you're among friends, immediately putting you in a more productive and lively frame of mind. It's the small things like a friendly hello in the morning that can start making a difference in how a team operates and how the team members interact with each other.

The advice in this shortcut can be applied to any team environment, but because Scrum teams are probably the most tight-knit groups that you will operate within (unless you are actually locking your head between two sweaty teammates' midriffs—yep, that is what an original rugby scrum is all about), it is even more important to ensure that everyone is feeling energized and excited about coming to work.

We are at work for most of our waking hours. We often spend more time with our colleagues then we do with our spouses and children. For those of you who just read that sentence and sighed profoundly, you need to read on, because coming to work should not be like entering the dark coalmines.

The good news is that it is extremely easy to implement some very simple (and inexpensive) measures to maintain team member satisfaction.

Individual Gratitude

After all of this Scrum talk promoting the centrality of the team, you might be feeling that individual recognition is a no-no. Scrum is certainly more focused on the achievements of the team than on those of the individual, but it does not mean that individuals simply become cogs in a machine. The fact remains that teams are made up of individuals, and individuals still maintain a sense of self-worth and appreciate having their hard work recognized.

I was the ScrumMaster in a new Scrum team that performed so well during a particularly critical project that we were recognized in the national companywide awards with the Team of the Year prize. This recognition was genuinely appreciated by the group, but it was obvious to me that each team member was much more appreciative when I personally went to each one of them and sincerely thanked them for a job well done, acknowledging specific contributions that they had made. Tony Schwartz, president and CEO of the Energy Project, blogs in the *Harvard Business Review*, comments on why individual appreciation matters so much:

> Feeling genuinely appreciated lifts people up. At the most basic level, it makes us feel safe, which is what frees us to do our best work. It's also energizing. When our value feels at risk, as it so often does, that worry becomes preoccupying, which drains and diverts our energy from creating value. (Schwartz 2012)

I'm certainly not recommending that the team shouldn't be thanked collectively, but as Dale Carnegie, author of *How to Win Friends and Influence People* (1981), poetically puts it, "leaving a friendly trail of little sparks of gratitude on your daily trips" certainly goes a long way.

Physical Environment

I remember a few years ago when an email illustrating the funky environment of the Google Zurich offices went viral ("Jobs at Google" 2005). I recall many of my non-software friends were incredulous at what they perceived to be capricious spending on furniture and fixtures that they claimed were more suited to a playground than a serious office. "Do they do any actual work there, or do they just goof around having fun all day?" an attorney buddy of mine bemoaned at the time.

Our industry is the leading light in guiding the corporate world out of the dark days of stark, gloomy offices that feel more like Industrial Age factories. Unlike my legal friend, many technology companies (in particular) understand that doing serious work while enjoying one's physical environment is actually possible!

Now I'm not saying that you need to go out and stock up on colorful beanbags, incandescent lava lamps, and slippery-slides. However, aiming to turn your physical working environment into something that feels a bit more like home shouldn't be viewed as capricious and whimsical but as a goal that just makes sense!

Scrum relies heavily on an interactive physical environment that promotes the Scrum value of openness, so the following list should be considered the basics for an environment conducive to Scrum:

- Plentiful whiteboard and wall space that can house the various task boards and associated artifacts.
- Plenty of light (although I have worked with the odd developer or two who had vampire tendencies and preferred the dark).
- Open desk space for each team, with partitions only to separate the different teams.
- Ample chair space to allow for comfortable walkthroughs (see Shortcut 12).
- A small, round discussion table for each team within its working area.
- Readily available, large meeting rooms with projectors and whiteboards for the Scrum meetings, such as sprint planning, reviews, and retrospectives.
- Do-not-disturb zones where team members can go to think in peace—this area should include a desk and some room to pace around.
- Private areas where personal phone calls can be made.
- Buffering from the noisier elements of the organization, such as the sales or customer service teams who typically talk on phones for much of the day.

Tools of the Trade

Offering developers the latest and greatest technology shouldn't be seen as a magnanimous gesture. Do you think carpenters see a sharp chisel as a privilege? No, they see it as a bare necessity to complete a professional job.

The funny thing is that, in my experience, developers who are offered their choice of the latest and greatest equipment see it as the most wonderful benefit. As the software commentator Joel Spolsky (2007) points out, "Programmers are easily bribed by giving them the coolest, latest stuff. This is a far cheaper way to get them to work for you than actually paying competitive salaries!" Now, I'm sure Joel is not advocating paying non-competitive salaries, but the point is that by simply providing the right tools for the job rather than maintaining traditional false economies (by offering old hand-me-down machines to save a couple of bucks), you are not only keeping developers happy but also improving overall productivity!

Identity

Humans are tribal by nature, and we like to feel that we are part of an elite group. Scrum lends itself nicely to allowing these social dynamics to develop, thanks particularly to the strong encouragement to collocate team members within the same contiguous area. Once this first step has been achieved, it's time to really build those strong bonds. I encourage (but certainly don't force) Scrum teams to adopt a name and a color, just as sports teams do, and to decorate their area with corresponding posters, logos, and banners. As Tom DeMarco and Timothy Lister point out in their landmark book *Peopleware* (1999), "Jelled teams are usually marked by a strong sense of identity . . . team members feel they're part of something unique. They feel they're better than the run of the mill."

In one company that I introduced Scrum to, we ended up with a Team Spitfire, Team Thundercats, and even a creatively named Team Awesome, all of whom waged friendly battle by constantly teasing each other for breaking the build or for having overly long daily scrums. I truly believe that this innocent competition improved productivity as well as pride in the quality of the work produced.

Although team identity is vital, it is also really important that the team identifies with and feels engaged with the product they are developing. As Cohn (2009) aptly puts it,

> One of the best ways of adding energy is increasing passion. The more passionate people are about their projects, the more likely they are to fully engage in them each day. The product owner is the key here. Product owners need to convey a compelling vision around the product being developed so that team members are enthusiastic about working on it.

A nice way that I have seen to help build this passion and sense of involvement is to include the developers in some of the early user story workshops so that they not only feel involved in the conception of the product but also get an early idea of what they will be expected to develop and why.

Shining Happy People

Making our working environment feel like home or, better yet, like an exciting amusement park (including the resident jokers and clowns—I've had plenty in my teams) perhaps takes us back to our most carefree times during childhood when we were arguably at our most creative and happy.

It is an illusion that it takes grandiose gestures such as bonuses, important-sounding job titles printed on delightfully watermarked business cards, or initiatives like Google's famed "20 percent time" (Wojcicki 2011) to keep people motivated. I don't even think it is critical that people feel a constant sense of "mastery, purpose, and autonomy," as written by Dan Pink in *Drive: The Surprising Truth about What Motivates Us* (2011), to feel productive and happy (although it certainly helps). Instead, a warm greeting in the morning, a sincere pat on the back for a task well done, and the feeling that you are part of a unique team can often be all that is required to maintain smiling faces.

Wrap Up

The three shortcuts discussed in this chapter focused on a selection of tactics, tools, and tips to help you and your organization get Scrum off the ground. Let's recap what was covered:

Shortcut 1: Scrum on the Pitch

- Scrum's elevator pitch.

- The concept of fixed flex, used to reduce context-switching while still offering scope flexibility.

- A range of key benefits relating to both the Scrum team and the project sponsors.

Shortcut 2: Fragile Agile

- How to differentiate between a framework and a method.

- Reasons it is more important to focus on an individual's qualities than on his or her qualifications.

- A selection of Scrum antipatterns to watch out for.

Shortcut 3: Creative Comfort

- Ways to improve team morale by focusing on team and individual appreciation.

- Ideas for improving the physical working environment to ensure a collaborative and productive space.

- Tips for helping your teams create a sense of identity and purpose.

Chapter 2
ATTITUDES AND ABILITIES

If you look at a typical classifieds list, it's evident that, when defining job roles, many organizations seem to place an overly significant emphasis on surface-level roles and responsibilities. For Scrum to succeed, it is imperative to take a different approach, delving deeper into the inherent and fundamental attitudes and abilities that are required of a Scrum team member.

The following three shortcuts will help you dig below the surface of these new roles to really appreciate what is required for a team member to excel.

Shortcut 4: Masterful ScrumMaster identifies seven key abilities that great ScrumMasters should possess. Shortcut 5: Rock Stars or Studio Musicians? focuses on a selection of attitudes that we should require of our team members. Finally, Shortcut 6: Picking Your Team Line-Up offers guidance on how best to assemble an effective working Scrum team.

Shortcut 4: Masterful ScrumMaster

I don't believe that the important ScrumMaster title should be bestowed on someone just because he or she knows the Scrum rules and practices back to front. Instead, this title should be granted only to those who genuinely understand and can bring to life the underlying ethos of the role. That is, a ScrumMaster should truly understand what it means to be a *servant-leader*. Robert Greenleaf, founder of the modern-day servant-leadership movement, describes this seemingly contradictory role:

> It begins with the natural feeling that one wants to serve, to serve first. Then conscious choice brings one to aspire to lead. That person is sharply different from one who is leader first, perhaps because of the need to assuage an unusual power drive or to acquire material possessions. (Greenleaf 2008)

So, what does servant-leadership entail in the context of Scrum? Well, let's look at some of the attitudes and abilities that should come naturally to a real-deal ScrumMaster.

Leading without Authority

The ability to lead without being bestowed butt-kicking privileges is the ultimate challenge for a new ScrumMaster. It is often hard to join a group, harder to lead a group, and hardest of all to lead a group without explicit authority (see Figure 2.1).

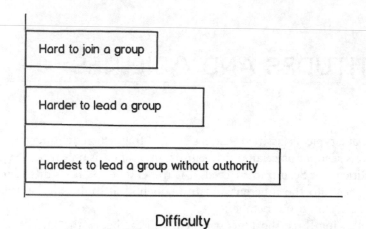

Difficulty

FIGURE 2.1   Leading without authority requires a genuine servant-leader.

Ruling with extreme authority may seem easy on the surface, but any toppled dictator would agree that it is not a sustainable long-term option. Although a dictator may force results for a period of time, without the respect of his or her followers, it is only a matter of time before the so-called leadership crumbles and chaos reigns, irrespective of the force used to maintain control. A truly respected leader requires no authority and certainly no force. People want to follow this person and are inspired by this more subtle brand of leadership.

I believe that this ability is innate, though perhaps hard to develop. For those who are not quite there but are willing to try, here is a shortlist of starting points:

- Drop the ego.
- Genuinely care about both the team and the product.
- Act fairly and consistently toward all team members.
- Exude confidence yet humbleness at the same time.
- Make yourself extremely approachable at all times (bathroom breaks are an exception!).

Bring about Change without Fear

As Woodrow Wilson, the twenty-eighth president of the United States, put it, "If you want to make enemies, try to change something" (Wilson 1916). Change is scary to most people; it takes them out of their comfort zones into a strange new world where their status and expertise are potentially under threat. The problem for the enthusiastic new ScrumMaster is that introducing Scrum will transform a project team's world. Even constructive change, when not handled carefully, can be viewed negatively by team members.

When joining a new Scrum team, you *should not* rush in and change everything at once. Be patient; observe the environment, the current practices, the individuals, the team, the technologies, and the broader organizational landscape. Be a fly on every wall, and talk to as many people as possible. Even if your mandate is to jump in and totally "scrummify" the place, first gauge the readiness of those who need to be involved. You get only one chance to make a first impression, so if you strike before the optimal time, enacting change becomes that much harder.

Find and foster allies as soon as possible. Those who have an early adopting mindset and are excited about positive change will prove invaluable in assisting you to embed new practices.

When you're ready, start slowly, and first implement one or two initiatives (perhaps introduce the daily scrum and a consolidated product backlog). Achieve a couple of small yet decisive victories, communicate the proven benefits, and build from there. Once you have established your credibility, the environment will be much more conducive to rapidly rolling out the rest of your initiatives.

Be Diplomatic without Being Political

The ScrumMaster is the hub connecting the spokes. These spokes are the previously disconnected departments that need to be brought together in perfect harmony to function as an effective Scrum team. More often than not, there will be a deeply entrenched silo mentality in place, separating the engineering team from the marketing team (see Figure 2.2). Worse than this is the sad fact that these silos are often more akin to fortresses, with barricades to keep the other "tribe" out. Breaking down this us-and-them mentality requires delicate diplomatic skills. It is about promoting broader team benefit and a healthy respect for all roles required to get the job done. The ScrumMaster should never take sides or get caught up in company politics—this

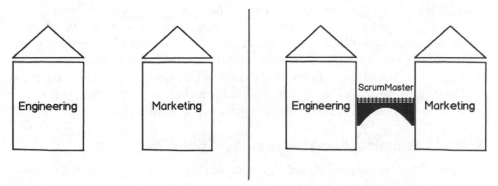

FIGURE 2.2   A great ScrumMaster will bridge the gap between departmental silos.

is about productivity and maintaining a healthy working environment—and as we all know, politicking is mutually exclusive to both of those goals. As Rubin writes:

> The ScrumMaster is transparent in all forms of communication. When working with team members there is no room for hidden agendas; what you see and hear from the ScrumMaster must be what you get. (Rubin 2012)

Behave Selflessly without Downplaying the Role

I remember watching the Tour de France (the annual, grueling 2,500-mile cycling race) and being amazed by the sprint finish of a particularly energy-sapping stage. After the speed picked up considerably, there was an almighty mess of bikes battling toward the line. With only a few miles to go, two riders from the same team broke out of the melee, one riding in relative safety on the back wheel of the first rider, who was forced to negotiate his way through the daunting impediments all around him. After doing all the hard work, the first rider slowed down and fell back into the rest of the peloton, having spent every ounce of his energy, leaving his teammate clear of the pack to take victory. This seemingly selfless role in a cycling team is performed by the *lead-out man*, whose duty is to use every last vestige of his endurance and tactical thinking to protect his teammate and guide him to victory without taking individual glory. A ScrumMaster needs to perform like a lead-out man; team recognition needs to be placed above his or her own. However, just because one is selfless, it doesn't mean that their pivotal role should be downplayed. Although the lead-out man (or woman) won't be standing high on the podium, the role he or she plays is recognized as absolutely vital to the team's success.

Protect without Being Overprotective

The metaphorical comparison that is commonly used when describing the role of the ScrumMaster is that of the sheepdog, guiding the flock through treacherous terrain and protecting them from hungry wolves. I like this comparison, but I also warn about taking this part of the function too far. A good ScrumMaster is careful about overassisting a team in the same way that a mom or dad (with all the very best of intentions) needs to be careful not to become a "helicopter parent"—constantly hovering and not giving the child a chance to solve his or her own problems.

The ScrumMaster needs to implicitly know when to jump in to aid the team and must also realize when it is okay just to sit back and let the team try to resolve their problems so that they can grow both personally and professionally.

Maintain Technical Knowledge without Being an Expert

Although technical experts can make great ScrumMasters, I often find that there are two big issues when the ScrumMaster is either a technical or domain expert:

- When a team member is stuck, it can be awfully tempting to jump in too early to help him or her resolve the problem.

- The desire will be strong to get overly involved in the technical/functional details within the sprint planning sessions (see Shortcut 8). In these situations, the ScrumMaster can potentially become distracted from the core facilitation responsibilities.

Be Comfortable Never Finishing

A ScrumMaster may reach a glorious day when he or she looks at the team and is tempted to say, "Wow, we totally rock! There really isn't anything more I can do to improve things here." No matter how well things are humming along, remember that achieving perfection is an impossible ambition, and improvements can always be made. Furthermore, a team will change over time, through natural attrition, promotion, and in some (unfortunate) cases expulsion, so when these dynamics change, there will be plenty of work to do and improvements to be made.

Next Generation Leadership

Genuine ScrumMasters form part of a new generation of enlightened professionals. The role of the ScrumMaster is deep and complex and should never be seen simply as a laundry list of operational functions—it is important to look deeper below the surface to find the foundational roots and understand what they are about.

Finally, I implore organizations to remain open-minded when trying to identify future ScrumMasters because they may originate from any background. They are people who can successfully demonstrate the abilities discussed in this shortcut, and although not everyone can be a ScrumMaster, a ScrumMaster can be anyone.

Shortcut 5: Rock Stars or Studio Musicians?

When no one is looking, I would really like to sneak one extra line into the Agile Manifesto:

We Prefer Attitude over Aptitude

That is, although there is value in aptitude, we value a great attitude more.

Don't get me wrong: aptitude is certainly important, but if I had to choose between a proficient developer with a super attitude and a genius developer with a surly attitude, I would choose the former over the latter.

Rock Stars

There is a movement in IT recruiting circles to try to locate "rock-star" developers. I've always had an issue with this juxtaposition because it sends a confused message to the market. Let's think about this for a minute: What are the qualities that are synonymous with rock stars? I'm sure you'll agree that rock stars are typically perceived as charismatic, creative, and individualistic—good traits, right? Flipping the coin now, let's look at some of the less laudable, stereotypical characteristics—think temperamental, attention-seeking, and arrogant, with a healthy dose of my-way-or-the-highway attitude thrown in. Does this sound like the type of person who would play nicely in a tight Scrum team? I think not.

Studio Musicians

Now, let's look at studio musicians. These musicians are happy to live out of the limelight and instead support the lead singer in producing a great album. As long-time music industry veteran Bobby Owsinski writes in *The Studio Musician's Handbook* (2009):

> Studio musicians are expected to be creative, be extremely versatile, and have a formidable skill set. . . . The fact that you are working very closely with other players, engineers, producers, artists, label and agency people (and who knows who else) usually means that the easier you are to work with, the more likely you'll get asked back.

> There's a way to do things in the studio, and it differs from playing live. A studio musician's protocol exists, and you'll be expected to abide by it. Suffice it to say that if you like being the center of attention, then studio work may not be for you.

My conclusion: I'd much rather have a team of studio musicians than a team of rock stars.

Scrum Values

How should you go about selecting a team of studio musicians to ensure that your scrum doesn't collapse under the weight of immense ego and constant bickering? The best place to start is with Scrum's core values, which should be embraced by all team members, forming the basis of their professional personality. These values are shown in Figure 2.3.

In addition to these values, I am always seeking the following attitudinal attributes in my Scrum team members: energy, empathy, curiosity, and friendliness. Let's explore what I mean in more detail.

FIGURE 2.3   Scrum's core values should be embraced by all team members.

Energy

I've worked with some really smart developers who were easygoing and friendly enough. Sounds like our type of candidate, right? Well, these same developers had special powers akin to those of the soul-sucking Dementors from Harry Potter.[1] Using their zombie-like interactions, these developers were somehow able to sap all positive energy from a room, especially during the daily scrums, where the aim is to set an energetic tone for the entire day. So, if any low-energy team members are dragging the rest of the group down, see if there is anything bothering them that you can help with.

Empathy

Working in a close team requires patience and understanding. Each team member is reliant on others to help achieve the collective goals, and the reality is that we are all prone to having off days. A flat tire, a late babysitter, difficult personal circumstances, or simply feeling unwell—any number of things can throw us off stride. When these situations inevitably arise, teammates are expected to step up to the plate and, if necessary, temporarily help carry any additional load in the same way that a fellow soldier will help stretcher a wounded comrade off the battlefield.

Curiosity

Development teams are cross-functional. As you'll read in Shortcut 6, these teams are ideally made up of members possessing "T-shaped" skills who have the ability to work adequately outside of their specialty when the need arises to help avoid bottlenecks. This requires team members to be willing and eager to extend their skill sets, taking every opportunity to learn more about the functions that they are not necessarily expert at.

Friendliness

I remember working with a somewhat antisocial yet highly intelligent developer who I felt needed a talking to after a particularly critical attack on a new product owner. Our conversation went something like this:

---

1. To learn more about Dementors, go to http://harrypotter.wikia.com/wiki/Dementor.

Me: "Irrespective of what you thought of his ideas, there are ways and means of communicating without resorting to verbal nuclear bombardment."

Him: "Well, I'm not being paid to make friends—I'm here to do a job."

Me: "Well, yes and no, pal. You're correct in that you are here to do a job; however, you are also being paid to work in a highly collaborative team environment. The more friendly you are, the more effective you will be."

Him: (Silence)

When selecting a team member, I'm not just looking for someone who is polite; I try to identify someone who is genuinely friendly. It is much easier to rally to a friend's aid than to a stranger's (or even worse, someone you dislike), and it goes without saying that working with friends is much more fun (and that can only be a good thing). As Jurgen Appelo, author of *Management 3.0* (2011), writes, "It doesn't mean you have to be close friends with everyone. That's not even possible. But simply knowing a little more about their life, their families, their home, and their hobbies (and them knowing some more about yours) would be a great start."

Respect

Respect is one of the core Scrum values mentioned earlier. I feel it is important to explain my interpretation of *respect* in more detail, because unlike the other Scrum values, its application can sometimes be ambiguous.

Let's face it: people (even very smart ones) occasionally come up with some less-than-stellar ideas. Perhaps they misinterpreted some fundamental input, or maybe they just got excited and blurted out what was on their mind without filtering it first. Unfortunately, I've worked in several environments where a brainstorming session ended up feeling like a cagey Olympic judo match, the participants cautiously waiting for each other to slip up so that they could throw their "opponent" across the room with a heavy dose of criticism.

Hostility is the last thing you want in a creative zone. Instead, a constant feeling of safety should be generated from the knowledge that teammates will be respectful even if they aren't particularly enamored with an idea or opinion. As Dale Carnegie (1981) writes, "Show respect for the other person's opinions. Never say, 'you're wrong.'" When people hear "you're wrong" too many times, their ideas (including the good ones) are likely to dry up pretty quickly (see Figure 2.4). There are far better ways of disagreeing without being disrespectful.

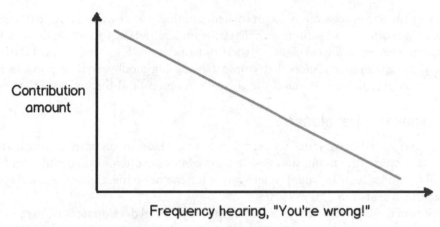

FIGURE 2.4   The effort you're willing to contribute goes down the more times you hear "You're wrong!"

Time to Make Music

I believe that Scrum's success is premised on the fact that you have a team with the same positive, collective attitude. A group of brilliant yet egotistical individuals will never work as well as a group of solid yet collaborative teammates.

Remember that Scrum is about the team, not the individuals. That doesn't mean individuals aren't recognized as unique and integral; however, it does mean that their personal goals should be superseded by those of the team. Owsinski (2009) writes

> Everyone is there to play their part as perfectly as possible. When the red light is off, the personalities are as diverse as you would see anywhere, but when it's time to make music, everyone's focus is 100% locked on the music.

Give me studio musicians over rock stars any day of the week, thank you very much!

Shortcut 6: Picking Your Team Line-Up

Sporting coaches deliberate for many months in anticipation of the annual draft pick, carefully considering whom they will target for potential inclusion on their teams. You're not always going to have the luxury of choice, however—just as when picking the line-up for a sports team, significant care must be taken when bringing your Scrum teams together. This is particularly pertinent if you are running a pilot project where the future of Scrum at your organization rests in the hands of a select few.

You must consider many factors when running your own Scrum "draft pick," including attitude, compatibility, skill sets, team size, ratio of functional specialties, shared resources, and workplace logistics, to name just a few. Most important is the selection of a team that is more than comfortable saying goodbye to their previous hierarchical team structures as well as the all too common us-and-them view of the world.

Everyone Is a Developer!

A successful, self-organizing Scrum team has no place for divisive, clannish structures that create functional silos within teams. Silos are often formed either on functional grounds (such as programmers versus testers) or on hierarchical grounds (such as technical leads versus non-leads).

Scrum combats this problem very simply: it views all development team members as equals and labels them accordingly with the collective title "developer." Whether you are a programmer, tester, user-experience designer, or technical writer, Scrum regards you as a developer. On a philosophical level, I really like this approach—it levels the playing field and reflects the fact that, to develop software, all functions need to participate (it isn't the sole domain of the programmer who previously monopolized the developer title).

In practice, this new vernacular can be a bit of a tough transition, so I like to frame it slightly differently. I explain to the team that it is like being a medical specialist; irrespective of specialty, all specialists are still doctors. In the same way that a doctor might specialize in neurology or pediatrics, a developer might specialize in programming or testing. I typically use the more specific "specialist" title (programmer, tester, etc.) when referring to developers for the sake of clarity, even though I certainly advocate the theoretical underpinnings of the broader developer title.

Scrum Team Size

I'll keep this next section short and sweet because there really isn't any contention in the community on this particular topic. As Mike Cohn confirms in his most recent book, *Succeeding with Agile* (2009), "The generally accepted advice is that the ideal Scrum team size is five to nine individuals." I'll simply add that my preference is for the lower side—typically five to seven.

Development Team Ratios

When it comes to determining the makeup of the development team, there is certainly no one-size-fits-all rule because every project and team is different. However, if you have no idea where to start, to get you going, I suggest a ratio that I have worked with successfully on multiple occasions (although I highly recommend that you inspect and adapt accordingly):

3 programmers : 1 tester : 0.5 "deep specialist(s)"

A few things to note:

- You may have multiple deep specialists working on a single Scrum team. By *deep specialists* I mean those who focus purely on niche areas, such as database administrators, user-experience designers, and subject-matter experts.

- 0.5 doesn't mean that I like working with pygmy specialists—it means that these developers split their time across two projects. We discuss this contentious suggestion a little more later in the shortcut.

- This ratio assumes a high level of test-automation maturity, leaving the tester to focus on the functions detailed in Shortcut 18.

With this ratio, I make mention of deep specialists. Although there is no problem including deep specialists in your Scrum teams, it is important to remember that Scrum is about finishing what is started as early as possible. To accomplish this type of flow, the concept of "swarming" is very important. Swarming means that rather than multiple developers working on several product backlog items (PBIs) at the same time, it is preferable to limit the work in progress and instead encourage as many developers as practicable to focus on completing a smaller number of PBIs. When deep specialists create a bottleneck because they are unavailable at critical junctures in a PBI's progress, the team faces a problem. To get the best of both worlds, I recommend encouraging developers to develop T-shaped skills (see Figure 2.5). As Kenneth Rubin (2012) explains, a developer who has T-shaped skills possesses deep vertical skills in a specialized area (such as user-experience design) as well as broad, but not necessarily deep, skills in other relevant areas (such as testing and technical writing). Team members with T-shaped skills better enable swarming behavior.

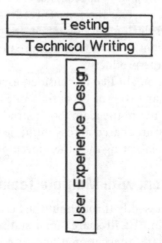

FIGURE 2.5   Encourage developers to have a deep specialty and multiple competencies.

Cohn (2009) recommends an approach that I've adopted to help nudge teams in the right direction:

> In your next sprint planning meeting, agree that one specialist on the team will not work in that specialty for the duration of the sprint. The specialist can advise others who do the specialty work but cannot do the work personally.

With receptive team members, the level of knowledge transfer will be very rapid, and although it might feel that the first couple of sprints are slow going, you will start seeing returns on this investment very soon after.

Fractional Assignment

In the previous section, I mentioned a 50 percent allocation for deep specialists. This "fractional assignment" is not overly popular across the Scrum community, and for good reason. James Shore and Shane Warden, authors of *The Art of Agile Development* (2007), put this down to the fact that

> fractional workers don't bond with their teams, they often aren't around to hear conversations and answer questions, and they must task switch, which incurs a significant hidden penalty.

I totally agree that ideally you want all team members dedicated 100 percent to the team. That being said, I have often found it unnecessary (from a requirement perspective) and unrealistic (from a budgeting perspective) to have deep specialists, such as database administrators, dedicated full time to a development team. That doesn't mean I disagree with Shore and Warden, nor does it mean there aren't occasions when you certainly need full-time deep specialists; however, it does mean that we often have to make the most of the skills available, and in many situations, we don't have the luxury of full-time deep specialists.

As a sort of consolation prize to the purists reading this book, I point out that although I am not against splitting developers across two projects, I am adamant that no one should ever be split across three or more projects—that level of context switching becomes very counterproductive.

Another option that you might like to consider, especially if a deep-specialist is required to work on more than two projects at the same time, is to treat them as consultants and trainers for the rest of the team. So, instead of including them as part of the actual Scrum team, they are shared across multiple teams and assist on specific tasks while at the same time educating the other developers.

Can a ScrumMaster Work with Multiple Teams?

I hear this debate waged incessantly throughout the Scrum forums and user groups. Before offering my viewpoint, I will share some statistics presented at the global Scrum Gathering (the primary international Scrum conference) by Scrum trainer Paul Goddard (2011):

- Seventy-five percent of ScrumMasters dedicate less than half of their time to being a ScrumMaster for their current team.

- Forty-five percent of ScrumMasters support two or more different Scrum teams.

- Eighty-eight percent of ScrumMasters take on additional responsibilities beyond that of a ScrumMaster.

Many in the Scrum community will strongly argue that the ScrumMaster role is significant enough to justify a "one team = one ScrumMaster" configuration. I support this argument, and Shortcut 26 highlights plenty of conclusive reasons demonstrating why being a ScrumMaster is absolutely a full-time role. That being said, it helps to remain open minded. I, for one, have acted as ScrumMaster on up to three teams at the same time, which, perhaps not ideal, can still work effectively assuming that the teams in question are well on their way to a mature state of self-organization. Let's explore this juggling act a little further.

First, brand-new Scrum teams require one full-time ScrumMaster—no question about it. These fresh teams require significant levels of education, guidance, assistance, and most of all, constant inspection and adaptation. Taking on more than one brand-new Scrum team is not at all realistic.

Maturing teams that are settling into Scrum successfully, without systemic impediments (such as ugly politics or similar issues), and who are trending positively on the continuous improvement scale can potentially manage with a ScrumMaster working across two different Scrum teams.

Finally, elite, mature Scrum teams that are truly self-organizing, where improvements are more about fine-tuning, can arguably get by with a ScrumMaster working across three similar Scrum teams (see Figure 2.6).

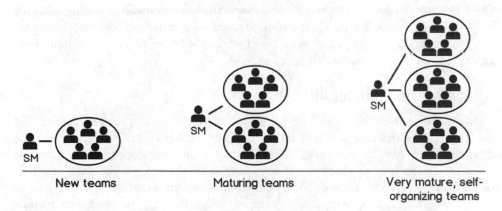

New teams   Maturing teams   Very mature, self-
organizing teams

FIGURE 2.6   Just how many teams a single ScrumMaster can handle depends on the maturity of the teams.

Attitude over Aptitude

Attitude is so important that I dedicated an entire shortcut to it, so instead of stealing my own thunder, I recommend that you read Shortcut 5.

Embrace Heterogeneity (But Beware)

Having had the opportunity to extensively travel and live on multiple continents, I can understand and appreciate the benefits that heterogeneity offers, and this is particularly evident when working in software teams. As software development is ostensibly a globally standardized industry, many of us have worked in environments that resemble the United Nations General Assembly.

Teams that consist of members from various cultural backgrounds, ages, experiences, and specialties are often far more interesting and end up forming environments that are breeding grounds for synthesizing novel solutions to problems.

But beware! In a few of the teams I've worked with, I had to sensitively break up some cultural cliques that had formed on the basis of geographical origin. The formation of cliques led to situations in which various languages (verbal, not programming) were being spoken in the open working area. Although it's human nature to gravitate toward people with whom you have much in common, I am very much against cultural cliques in a Scrum team setting. It causes feelings of exclusion, not to mention the potential lost knowledge-sharing due to others not comprehending the various questions being asked.

In addition, I have found that with diverse groups, team members need to be careful about sharing insensitive jokes and idle banter that might cause unintentional offense.

Household Rules

Lyssa Adkins, author of *Coaching Agile Teams* (2010), recommends forming what she calls "rules for living together" for handling scenarios similar to those just detailed.

For example, on one of the teams that I worked with, we had a set of "household rules" (see Figure 2.7) that we all followed.

All for One and One for All!

I always notice the magic moment when I'm working with a team and realize that no longer am I among a group of individuals but a cohesive, tightly knit team. The moment when this "jigsaw puzzle" clicks into place sometimes occurs when everyone is involved in an intense yet convivial discussion about the project, but often, it simply occurs when everyone is having some fun, enjoying a communal laugh over a joke or two. Seeing that gel form is my favorite moment—it is then that the Musketeer attitude truly appears, with all members of the team genuinely feeling they are in the same boat, knowing and believing they will win or lose together as a team (Rubin 2012).

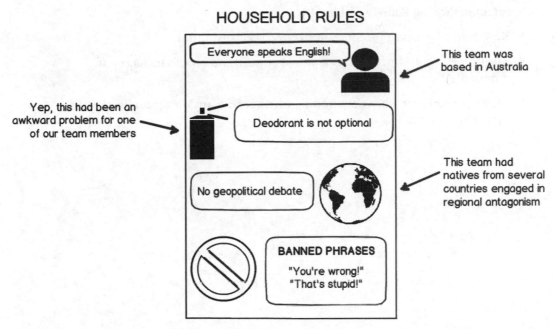

FIGURE 2.7   Prominently displaying your household rules reminds team members how they should treat each other.

Wrap Up

The three shortcuts discussed in this chapter focused on a selection of tactics, tools, and tips to help you and your organization appreciate the underlying attitudes and abilities required for a team to perform efficiently—even exceptionally. Let's recap what was covered:

Shortcut 4: Masterful ScrumMaster

- What it takes to be a genuine servant-leader

- The key abilities required of a great ScrumMaster

- The innate attitudes demonstrated by a true ScrumMaster

Shortcut 5: Rock Stars or Studio Musicians?

- The potential issues with rock star developers

- Why we want our developers to think and behave more like studio musicians

- A selection of values that should form your team's professional personality

Shortcut 6: Picking Your Team Line-Up

- Recommended development team size and specialist ratios

- The problem with fractional assignment of work and how to manage it if required

- Factors to consider when determining whether a ScrumMaster can work with more than one team

Chapter 3

PLANNING AND PROTECTING

Now that your organization is eager to adopt Scrum and a team has been selected with the right attitudes and abilities, it is time to snap into action and get the show on the road.

The following three shortcuts not only help you to set the team on their course but also give you some tips and tricks to keep the project on track.

Shortcut 7: Setting the Scrum Stage lays down a range of suggestions to ensure proper foundations have been established to support a successful Scrum team. Shortcut 8: Plan the Sprint, Sprint the Plan provides specific, practical advice to ensure an effective sprint planning session. Finally, Shortcut 9: Incriminating Impediments offers advice to help control the impact of impediments during sprint execution.

Shortcut 7: Setting the Scrum Stage

Scrum teams require chemistry, and just as in a science lab, successful "chemical reactions" are much easier to trigger when the broader organization provides the suitable ingredients and environment to work with. As Mike Cohn (2009) astutely recognizes, "The changes required to reap all of the rewards being agile can bring are far reaching. These changes demand a great deal from not only the developers but the rest of the organization as well."

Let's examine some of the key organizational and environmental preconditions that should ideally be considered as part of your Scrum adoption plan.

Ensure Team Stability

Tom DeMarco and Timothy Lister (1999) identify a key mantra that any organization seeking close-knit teams should adopt: "Preserve and protect successful teams."

I am comfortable admitting that I have worked on Scrum projects that I would consider to be less than successful. I can easily pinpoint the core reason for these subpar results: my inability as a ScrumMaster to keep the team together for the duration of the project. This problem often occurs when key developers are dragged off one project to work on a more urgent project (see Figure 3.1). Couple this problem with continual corporate restructuring (that seems to be happening more and more in these times of global financial difficulty), and it can be challenging to preserve great teams.

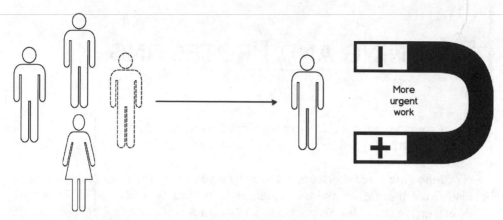

FIGURE 3.1   Beware of "more urgent" projects trying to drag team members away.

DeMarco and Lister (1999) also quantified the damage caused when rotating staff, concluding that "a reasonable assessment of startup cost (for a new team member) is therefore approximately three lost work-months per new hire." This estimate doesn't even take into account the less tangible costs such as lost momentum, damage to morale, and loss of valuable, tacit knowledge.

Adjust the Physical Environment

Without question, some of my most successful Scrum projects were those in which I was able to physically separate the Scrum teams from the rest of the organization.

DeMarco and Lister (1999) surmise why this may be the case:

> It almost always makes sense to move a project . . . out of corporate space. Work conducted in ad hoc space has got more energy and a higher success rate. People suffer less from noise and interruption and frustration.

I've worked with Scrum teams that had to operate in large, open spaces near the sales team who were frantically on their phones all day, every day. I've also had teams that had been hamstrung by the corporate facilities department who wouldn't allow them to move a small, measly round meeting table into their areas. I could go on and on, but the bottom line is that separation and environmental independence is the holy grail.

Irrespective of whether you are able to reach this lofty goal, you should do everything in your power to ensure that the Scrum team sits together. Scrum can certainly work for distributed teams where collocation isn't possible, but it's not optimal.

Apart from the obvious daily logistical benefits that sitting in close proximity offers, James Shore and Shane Warden (2007) offer an even more important rationale for the collocation of the team: "Sitting together is the most effective way I know to build empathy. Each group member gets to see that the others are working just as hard." Shortcut 3 goes into more detail regarding other key inclusions to incorporate into the physical working environment to ensure a physical space conducive to Scrum.

Estimates Are Not Guarantees

How is this for an infuriating scenario? The project sponsor casually strolls over to a team member and asks how long feature XYZ is going to take. The team member takes off her headphones, breaking focus from what she was working on, glances up and throws out a rough estimate to appease the sponsor. Lo and behold, the estimate proves to be inaccurate. The sponsor then applies immense pressure on the entire team to deliver on the promised "commitment," and dammit, if that means missing your kid's end-of-year concert, then that's the price of sticking to commitments!

News flash: An estimate is not a guarantee. If it were, there would be no need for the word. An estimate is simply a prediction based on known information and input at a given point in time. This definition needs to be clearly understood by the project stakeholders before the project kicks off!

Work toward Reciprocity

Mary and Tom Poppendieck, authors of *Leading Lean Software Development*, put forward the notion that there are two kinds of companies in this world: remuneration companies and reciprocation companies:

> People who work in a remuneration company have this agreement with their company: "I will show up for work and you will pay me for my time. If you want more than that, pay me more." On the other hand, people who work in a reciprocity company have this agreement: "I will treat you the way you treat me. I expect fair compensation, but if you want care and commitment on my part, then you agree that you will demonstrate care and commitment toward me, and you will help me develop my potential to its fullest extent." (Poppendieck and Poppendieck 2009)

The best Scrum teams consist of committed and caring individuals, so it naturally follows that companies that embrace the reciprocity model are more likely than remuneration companies to have greater success with Scrum, especially in the long term.

Support Sustainable Development

Shortcut 1 mentioned that one of Scrum's guiding principles is that team members should work at a sustainable pace.

In *Agile Product Management with Scrum,* Roman Pichler (2010) points out that

developing a product is like running a marathon. If you want to finish, you have to choose a steady pace. Many product owners make the mistake of pressuring the team to take on more work.

Any organization that maintains a culture of late-night martyrdom and continues to not only respect but also explicitly reward ludicrous overtime is at conflict with one of the principles of Scrum (or any other agile framework, for that matter). Overtime should be the exception, not the rule, and as recognized by Kent Beck in *Extreme Programming Explained* (1999), it should be recognized as "a symptom of a serious problem on the project," not simply business as usual.

Run a Pilot Project

Although there are certainly some advantages to taking the Big Bang approach to rolling out Scrum across an organization, I don't advocate it. Instead, I'm a big believer in initially running a pilot project. I recommend this approach even if the business is champing at the bit to roll Scrum out en masse. Why do I recommend investing this additional time if not to help obtain validation and buy-in? Mike Cohn (2009) explains the reason perfectly:

> [A] pilot project is undertaken to provide guidance to subsequent projects; it pilots the way in doing something new. . . . As an industry we have enough evidence that Scrum works; what individual organizations need to learn is how to make Scrum work inside their organizations.

I always run pilot projects before rolling out across a broader group, and in fact, without the experimental freedom that a pilot project offers, I'm not sure if you would even be reading this book today!

It may be tempting to select a project to pilot that is low value and therefore low risk. This is a false economy. Shore and Warden (2007) reinforce this point:

> Avoid taking a project with low value as a "learning opportunity." You'll have trouble involving customers and achieving an organizational success. Your organization could view the project as a failure even if it's a technical success.

Regarding team stability and the less-than-successful projects I experienced: the reason I couldn't keep those teams together was that the pilot projects we were working on were not of high enough priority and value. When push came to shove and shared resources were being stretched between the pilot project and the "more important" projects, no guesses as to which lost out.

How long should a pilot project last? Well, if you've been reading this section carefully, you will conclude that your pilot project should be no different from any other important project. As Roman Pichler (2010) states, "There is no rule in Scrum that mandates how long a project can last. But, it is common for agile projects to take no longer than three to six months."

Have Realistic Expectations

Change takes time, and very often with change, we need to take one step back to take two forward. Adopting Scrum requires a significant shift in organizational mindset that includes breaking entrenched habits, and this feat doesn't happen overnight.

There is going to be lead time before the developers feel comfortable working in cross-functional teams and before the old command-and-control attitudes disappear. Based on this premise, the organization should not be naïve and expect amazing gains immediately. Patience and nurturing is the name of the game, and a supportive organization will no doubt see its investment reaping dividends in the near future.

Shortcut 8: Plan the Sprint, Sprint the Plan

As one of the "elements of a chemistry-building strategy for healthy organizations," DeMarco and Lister (1999) recommend providing "lots of satisfying closure." I totally agree with their advice and suggest another complementary element: the provision of lots of clean, fresh starts. Luckily for us, the sprint time-box offers both closure and fresh starts, and in this shortcut we explore the Scrum activity that offers us the regular fresh start: *sprint planning*.

By collectively resetting the goals for the upcoming sprint every few weeks, the team can start afresh rather than remain stuck on a seemingly endless treadmill of ongoing work. Further, without this regular and expected planning session, significant disruption is caused when team members are rounded up on an ad hoc basis to plan and design.

Product Backlog Refinement

Before the team is gathered in the planning room, I recommend a few preliminary steps to ensure that the product backlog is refined appropriately. First, ensure that the product owner (with relevant assistance) not only has determined the next priority requirements for the upcoming sprint but also has fleshed them out in just enough detail to allow the developers to get started. Doing so might mean including more detailed acceptance criteria as well as any wireframes or mock-ups if applicable (see Shortcut 11). Additionally, it helps if the product owner has taken some time to collaborate in advance with any specialist testers to develop a set of initial test cases (based on the acceptance criteria) to fully describe the inner workings of the required functionality.

Goals Are Good

I would say that most of us enjoy working toward goals, so it is helpful to determine a centralized sprint goal that is omnipresent throughout the sprint. This focal goal typically maps to the main theme of the sprint. For example, the sprint goal might be *Enhance the Messaging Engine*; this doesn't mean that other bits and pieces can't also be worked on during the sprint, but it does indicate that the majority of the work will target the messaging engine. A sprint goal also helps with decision making by ensuring that everyone remains focused rather than deviating and heading off on tangents.

How Long Should a Sprint Be?

Back in the day, it was recommended that the sprint duration should be 30 days—no more, no less. These days, things have become somewhat more flexible, and it is now pretty much universally accepted that the sprint length can vary from team to team. If you speak to any Scrum team, you will find that the vast majority of sprints run from 1 to 4 weeks. I have tried them all out, and in my opinion, 1 week is too short, 4 weeks is too long, leaving me sitting on the fence between 2 and 3 weeks. For a new project, I make the decision based on two factors:

- **Team preference:** Some people prefer the longer duration to help gain more momentum, whereas others prefer the simpler planning that a shorter sprint offers.

- **Volatility of requirements:** If the product owner is likely to change requirements more often than not due to the product domain or market conditions, then I definitely recommend the shorter duration (see Figure 3.2).

Now, an important point: When the preferred sprint length is confirmed (it may take some experimenting in the early days), it should be locked in and rarely changed. There are specific reasons to avoid sporadically adjusting the sprint length, including the following:

- For team focus, a regular rhythm helps the team better understand how to pace itself.

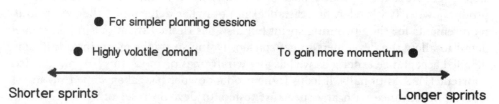

FIGURE 3.2 Factors to take into account when considering sprint length.

- The velocity metric (see Shortcut 13) relies on a consistent sprint duration; otherwise, it becomes less meaningful and more difficult to calculate.

- If you change the duration of sprints, your sprint review, retrospective, and planning sessions will not fall on the same day of the week. Such irregularities can prove to be a logistical headache, especially if you have to share meeting rooms with others in the organization.

Capacity Planning

Before diving into the sprint planning process, the team needs to first determine its sprint capacity. First, remember that not everyone will have full capacity for every sprint. Some team members may need to work across multiple projects—certainly not an ideal situation, but it can happen (see Shortcut 6). If this is the case, make sure that these developers aren't overallocated. Also, don't forget to take into account any public holidays, training, or scheduled leave.

Second, don't fall into the trap of believing that those who are dedicated full time to the sprint will be able to spend their entire working day on sprint-related tasks.

For example, in a team that I recently worked with (using 2-week sprints), a full-time developer was typically allocated a capacity of 9 days × 6 hours per day = 54 hours per sprint to work on tasks.

First, we used 9 days because the equivalent of 1 full day was dedicated to the sprint planning, review, and retrospective sessions. Six hours a day was allocated because in a typical 8-hour day we found that an individual would usually get only about 6 hours of solid sprint-focused work. The rest of the time was often taken up by various other activities unrelated to the current sprint, such as refining the product backlog (in anticipation for the upcoming sprint) and more general tasks required to be a good citizen of the organization (such as responding to email and assisting others not in the Scrum team). Please note that the proposed capacity per day will vary depending on the team and environment. As such, 6 hours a day should not be considered a universal standard, and I recommend using historical sprint interference statistics (see Shortcut 19) to help you determine your team's estimated sprint capacity.

Let's now take a look at the flow of the actual sprint planning session, which I like to split into two distinct parts:

Part 1: The What

This segment is all about the product owner presenting the next-highest-priority product backlog items (PBIs) to the development team as well as fielding any specific questions. This task is conducted for each of the PBIs that are being targeted for completion in the upcoming sprint. I recommend using the team's velocity (see Shortcut 13) as a rough guide to determine how many PBIs the product owner should be prepared to run through during this session.

Part 2: The How

Moving on, it is then time for the development team to break the PBIs into more granular technical tasks and to estimate each task to the nearest hour. Although estimating in hours may still be inaccurate at times, it helps the team make more informed design trade-off decisions and assists in establishing more confidence in what will likely be delivered by the end of the sprint. As Cohn (2007) explains further:

> The goal is not the hours but the hours are often a good tool to use to ensure we have discussed things (mostly the technical and product design of those things) at a level sufficient to enter the sprint with a good feeling that we'll be able to finish all the work of the sprint.

I don't expect product owners to hang around for this second part (unless they particularly want to). That being said, I stipulate that although product owners don't necessarily need to be in the room, they certainly need to be on call in case any further clarification is required. Nothing stalls a sprint planning session more than an unavailable product owner!

Even though I like to use velocity-based planning as a guide for Part 1, I like to also use what is commonly known as *commitment-based planning* to determine the number of specific tasks to include in the sprint backlog. Here are the steps that the development team typically runs through during commitment-based planning:

1. Start with the highest-priority PBI.

2. Deconstruct the PBI into tasks with estimates in hours.

3. Identify any specific task dependencies.

4. Continue this cycle until the team's collective capacity is full.

5. If the output from the velocity-based approach (from Part 1) doesn't match the output from the commitment-based approach, simply call back the product owner (if she has left the room) to add additional PBIs (if there is still capacity) or explain to her why there will be fewer PBIs targeted than initially expected (if the capacity is filled earlier than initially expected).

Task Definition

I typically set a few parameters for the generation of tasks:

- Each task needs to be a small, testable slice of the overall PBI (see Shortcut 10) and needs to factor in all activities required to meet the task's definition of "done" (see Shortcut 11).

- Each task should take no longer than about 8 hours (the shorter, the better, though).

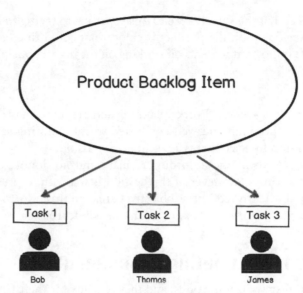

FIGURE 3.3 Although a single PBI can be worked on by multiple developers, each task should be worked on by only one developer.

- Although more than one developer can work on a single PBI, there should be only one developer (or developer pair) working on a task (see Figure 3.3).

- Don't forget to include tasks for the sprint review preparation (see Shortcut 22), such as preparing demo data if required.

You now have the sprint backlog compiled, including the tasks and corresponding estimates for them. The original estimates for the tasks can be aggregated to form the sprint's initial remaining time, and this time can then be recalculated each day and tracked on the sprint burndown chart (see Shortcut 19). Before going home each day, everyone on the development team should adjust the remaining time for any tasks they had been working on that day to ensure that up-to-date data is being fed into the sprint burndown chart.

The Right Number of Requirements

In a perfect world, after sprint planning is all said and done, you will have a nice neat whole number of PBIs that the team anticipates it will be able to complete in the forthcoming sprint. What you will find occasionally is that there will be a small amount of expected capacity left over that isn't quite enough to fit a whole new PBI into. That's okay—simply acknowledge as a team that the intention is to commence the next-highest-priority requirement without setting the expectation that it will be completed by the end of the sprint. I prefer this approach to trying to identify a small enough PBI (lower down on the product backlog) that could fit in nicely because I feel that it is more important to focus on working on the highest business value items.

The 7 Ps

As the British army adage goes, "Proper planning and preparation prevents piss-poor performance," so a thorough and well-conducted sprint planning session is important to help generate a forecast that is as accurate as possible.

The sprint won't always go according to plan, and no doubt adjustments will need to be made at times. However, if this session is well run, everyone will have a much better idea of what the collective objectives are, and this information will make the coordination and alignment of expectations a great deal easier.

Shortcut 9: Incriminating Impediments

You've trained your new Scrum troops, and they're ready for their first mission. The team is pumped, and the project is up and running. Things are going well; the daily scrums are happening, the continuous integration server is humming along, tasks are moving across the board, so life is pretty sweet. Then, from out of nowhere, the bullets start flying, the mines start exploding, and your troops are no longer moving forward. This is it, ScrumMaster—time to step up!

Okay, so perhaps in reality, it isn't a spray of enemy fire impeding your team. Instead, it might be a constantly breaking build, an interfering project sponsor, or perhaps the loss of a key team member. The bottom line is that anything impeding your team's progress becomes the number-one priority for the ScrumMaster to tackle.

Defining Impediments

Let's start by defining what an *impediment* is. Here is the definition I choose to use:

> An event that impedes any of the developers from working to their anticipated sprint capacity.

If you recall from Shortcut 8, it isn't wise to allocate a full-time developer a sprint capacity of 8 hours a day (for a typical 8-hour working day). *Why not?* you ask. Well, you have to be realistic: there is no way that people are going to spend every second of their operational time working on their sprint tasks. We must take into account the various meetings that will pop up, other extended collaboration time, unplanned company events, and important head-clearing breaks, just to name a few. Now don't get me wrong: on some days, some team members will be able to maintain strong focus on their sprint tasks and will max out or even exceed the 8 hours. However, on other days, constant interruptions may make it difficult to maintain even a couple of hours of sprint-focused work.

Many Shapes and Sizes

Impediments come in all shapes and sizes. Following is a small sample of indicative impediments (both operational and systemic) to keep a careful eye on:

- **Meetings of large magnitude:** Scrum projects really should have no need for these extraneous, long-winded bad boys, so when they pop up, they are typically triggered by other areas of the business or by unforeseen issues.

- **Illness:** Illness can strike unannounced at any time. Not much you can do about it, but I highly recommend you avoid a culture of "toughing it out" when sick. That expectation is just stupid. Work quality suffers, germs spread very quickly in an open Scrum environment, and it just annoys everyone.

- **Broken builds:** Without a healthy build (see Shortcut 18), development cannot continue. If a build is broken, it must be the top priority of every team member to fix it.

- **Issues with the tools of the trade:** Whether it is a hardware malfunction, software problem, or network connectivity issues, any problems with the working environment can seriously hamper progress and lead to immense frustration.

- **Unreliable supplier:** This is possibly one of the most frustrating impediments due to the lack of control that the ScrumMaster and team might have in dealing with an overburdened supplier. Poorly supported components or add-ons can lead to black holes that can seriously suck time from your sprints.

- **Unrefined product backlog:** A sprint should never start without the product owner knowing exactly what requirements should make their way into the sprint backlog. Further, these requirements should include enough detail for the development team get their teeth into. If these requirements are not ready for the sprint planning session then the sprint will not start smoothly at all (see Shortcut 11).

- **Absent or unempowered product owner holding up key decisions:** Product owners should be available throughout the sprint to field specific questions about the sprint backlog. If they are regularly absent or constantly having to seek approval from elsewhere, the development team might find itself paralyzed with uncertainty.

- **Incentive schemes focused on the individual:** Many organizations maintain performance reviews (and associated incentive schemes) that are based entirely on individual performance. Hopefully by now you've absorbed the fact that there is no "I" in "Scrum team," so unless reviews also incorporate a significant focus on team collaboration, the organization will be sending a contradictory message to the team members.

Impediment ConTROL

I like to run through the following five-step approach when dealing with impediments: confirm, triage, remove, outline, learn (ConTROL).

- **Confirm:** Obviously it is necessary to confirm what the impediment is. Typically, impediments are raised in the daily scrum, but urgent impediments should be raised in real time rather than waiting for the daily scrum. The sprint retrospective can uncover further impediments that may have slipped through the cracks during the actual sprint. All impediments should be tracked and monitored until they are resolved.

- **Triage:** If you are bombarded with simultaneous impediments, then unless you are Superman (being obsessed with super heroes doesn't automatically give you their special powers), you will be able to tackle only one or two at a time. An impact and urgency assessment may be needed to help you determine where to start.

- **Remove:** Ideally, the Scrum team can remove any impediment that gets thrown its way, but it isn't always the reality. To avoid delays, it is important to know when to seek further help from other groups to get things back on track (see Shortcut 26).

- **Outline:** Both the Scrum team and stakeholders should be made aware of any impediments as they come up. You especially want to avoid surprises for product owners (and project sponsors) when it comes to any scuttled plans so that they have as much time as possible to iron out any cascade effects.

- **Learn:** The sprint retrospective (see Shortcut 23) is the main session during which impediments are analyzed. It is important to learn from these issues to avoid their recurrence and/or capture how they were dealt with so that if they strike again, the impact is less pronounced.

Blocks versus Impediments

Many teams use the terms *block* and *impediment* interchangeably, but I like to differentiate between the two (see Figure 3.4). I do so to clearly identify an obstruction that has *stopped* progress on a particular task but hasn't necessarily slowed down overall progress (a block) versus an obstruction that is *slowing down* the team's sprint progress (an impediment).

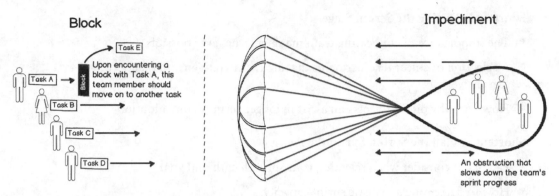

FIGURE 3.4   A block affects only a single task, whereas an impediment acts like a parachute, slowing down overall progress.

A typical block occurs when a task has a dependency that has been held up for some reason. A short, temporary block is a reasonably common occurrence and nothing to get too concerned about, because in most cases, other work can be taken on while the dependency is being taken care of. The important thing to note is that you want clear visibility of all blocked tasks, irrespective of how temporary the block may be. The way I like to track blocked tasks is to simply spin the corresponding sticky-note 45 degrees so that it looks like a diamond and stands out on the task board. This is a clear signal and allows you to immediately jump into detective mode to ensure that the block is removed as quickly as possible.

Understand the Terrain

If you're like me, you will be stunned when you think back to all of the impediments that occurred throughout a project. It is often only when you reflect on the compiled list of tracked impediments that you can really appreciate the difficult terrain your Scrum troops have had to negotiate.

This impediment list can also prove invaluable if ever you must defend the team should it fall under an uncomfortable spotlight due to incremental delays that have started to impact release dates. I certainly found that if you carefully ConTROL impediments when they decide to rear their ugly heads, these uncomfortable situations will be few and far between.

Wrap Up

The three shortcuts discussed in this chapter focused on a selection of tactics, tools, and tips to help you to set your team on course and keep them on track. Let's recap what was covered:

Shortcut 7: Setting the Scrum Stage

- The importance of collocating team members whenever possible

- A selection of cultural adjustments that are required to ensure that Scrum can thrive

- How and why pilot projects can assist in longer-term Scrum adoption

Shortcut 8: Plan the Sprint, Sprint the Plan

- Factors to consider when selecting your sprint length and goal

- How to determine a realistic sprint capacity

- Options for structuring your sprint planning session

Shortcut 9: Incriminating Impediments

- Definitions of impediments and blocks

- Types of impediments to watch out for

- How to ConTROL your list of impediments

Chapter 4

REQUIREMENT REFINEMENT

Thankfully, we no longer rely on the old practice of crystal-ball gazing to define an upfront "spec." That being said, the communication and validation of requirements can still be a challenging matter.

This chapter's three shortcuts guide your team in forming and monitoring both its requirements and the associated definition of done (DoD).

Shortcut 10: Structuring Stories provides recommendations on how teams may split their sprint-ready requirements into actionable tasks. Shortcut 11: Developing the Definition of Done offers food for thought to help the Scrum team establish and evolve the DoD. Finally, Shortcut 12: Progressive Revelations focuses on how your team can eliminate waste by conducting walkthroughs.

Shortcut 10: Structuring Stories

Although Scrum does not prescribe the use of any specific format to articulate the user requirements that appear as product backlog items (PBIs), I think it is safe to say that the user story format popularized by Mike Cohn's seminal book, *User Stories Applied* (2004), has become the de facto standard.

I would hazard a guess that anyone reading this book has read *User Stories Applied* and/or worked with the now ubiquitous format:

"As a . . . I want to . . . so that I can. . . ."

This shortcut isn't going to retread old ground and explore topics such as the benefits of user stories or how to split big stories into smaller stories—these topics are covered perfectly well by Cohn in *User Stories Applied*, so go check it out if you haven't already. Instead, I want to delve deeper into some user story aspects with less commentary surrounding them, such as the relationship between tasks and stories as well as how to handle "technical stories."

Breaking It Down

Apart from the typical, sprint-ready user story (see Shortcut 11), there are two other commonly used constructs to help us piece together requirements: epic stories and tasks.

Starting with the largest, Cohn (2009) describes an epic story as "A user story that will take more than one or two sprints to develop and test." When you are initially formulating your product backlog, the reality is that most of the requirements may well be more epic in nature. Remember that in Scrum, requirements are emergent, so it is not necessary to have detailed user stories for every requirement right from the beginning—only the top-priority items that are going to be worked on in the next one or two sprints need detailed user stories.

To split epics into sprint-ready user stories (our next level), I again refer you to Cohn's *User Stories Applied* (2004), where you will read about a range of options, including splitting by subactivity, subrole, data boundaries, and operational boundaries (among several others).

Tasks make up the third and most granular level, and once they are identified and defined (hopefully by using some of the suggestions we discuss in the next section), the team is ready to start building some great software!

Task Slicing and Dicing

Formulating feasible, sprint-ready user stories is only part of the challenge. What comes next for these top priority stories is a trip to the sprint planning session (see Shortcut 8) where they will become sprint backlog items.

The sprint backlog is typically made up of not only the nominated sprint-ready stories but also their offspring (generated during the sprint planning process), typically referred to as *tasks*. These are the specific, granular pieces of the story that are worked on by members of the development team during the sprint and are often tracked with colored sticky-notes on the task board (see Shortcut 21). I prefer that these tasks take between 2 and 8 hours. Any longer and they start to become unwieldy.

While splitting epic stories into sprint-ready stories can be considered an art form, the slicing and dicing of stories into specific tasks requires the talents of a well-trained sashimi chef!

A common task breakdown that I've seen (and have used in the past) goes something like this:

User Story

"As a new user, I would like to sign up to XYZ website so that I can start using its awesome services."

Task 1: Design end-to-end functional tests.

Task 2: Generate test data.

Task 3: Develop database layer.

Task 4: Develop business logic layer.

Task 5: Develop user interface layer.

Task 6: Develop end-to-end functional automation test.

I know this breakdown seems logical and straightforward, and it can work out just fine, but do you know what it looks like to me? Yep, you guessed it—a mini-waterfall! Although not nearly as dangerous as the scarier product-level waterfall approach, this mini version can still give us the same headaches, albeit on a more micro level. Focusing specifically on tasks 3, 4, and 5, it is evident that the product owner will find it difficult to verify and validate the requirement until all three of these tasks have been completed. Asking the product owner to verify the database schema changes and related stored procedures (task 3) won't necessarily provide reassurance that the development is heading in the right direction (as far as the user functionality is concerned).

Instead, why not also apply, down at a task level, the "vertical slice" mindset that is commonly utilized at a story level? By doing so, it becomes possible to start validating work in a matter of hours—how cool is that?

Now let's look at a vertical slice option that could be employed when breaking up the story into constituent tasks:

User Story

"As a new user, I would like to sign up to XYZ website so that I can start using its awesome services."

Task 1: Develop username/password functionality (including test design and automation).

Task 2: Develop email authentication functionality (including test design and automation).

Task 3: Develop landing page functionality (including test design and automation).

What I've done here is break up the story into some relatively encapsulated end-user functions, each incorporating a small amount of database work, business logic, and user interface implementation (see Figure 4.1). The best thing is that the mini-waterfall has now become a safe trickle, and the feedback loops can be measured in hours rather than days!

I'm sure one or two of you must be thinking as you read this, "Hang on a second—if you have managed to thin-slice this story into smaller functions, then why not make these functions into separate stories rather than tasks?" Well, that is a good question, and luckily I have a couple of answers. First, remember Cohn's advice: "The key is that stories should be written so that the customer can value them" (2004). Referring to the example above, although signing up for the website is certainly something that the customer can value, using a standalone email authentication function is not necessarily of value.

The second answer comes down to story independence. If you can split a story into smaller ones and it is possible to independently prioritize them, it makes sense to

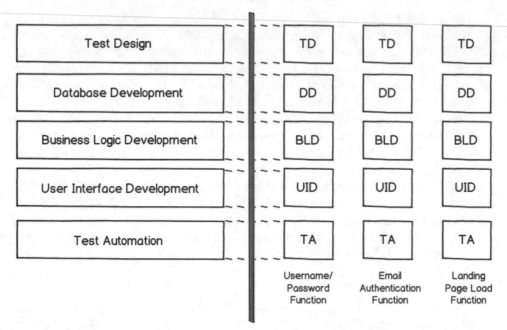

FIGURE 4.1   Instead of discrete layers, each task is vertically sliced to shorten feedback loops.

treat them as actual stories rather than tasks. Referring again to the example, I would argue that none of the tasks can be separately prioritized because the functionality that the customer values would be incomplete and incoherent.

Instead of eating our cake in layers, let's eat it in tasty slices so that we can enjoy everything the cake has to offer in one go!

Technical Stories and Bugs

I like Henrik Kniberg's straightforward definition of technical stories from his book *Lean from the Trenches* (2011):

> Technical stories are things that need to get done but that are uninteresting to the customer, such as upgrading a database, cleaning out unused code, refactoring a messy design, or catching up on test automation for old features.

I hear two common questions when it comes to technical stories:

- How can we write technical stories when user stories are supposed to be user-centric?

- How can we represent technical stories using the typical user story format?

My answer to the first question is that, wherever possible, instead of writing independent technical stories, try to represent the technical requirement as tasks within one of the functional user stories that is reliant on this technical work. Remember to ensure that if more than one functional story relies on the technical work, you factor in the tasks only once and in the story that has the highest priority.

I like the option of including technical work within functional stories (rather than as separate technical stories), primarily to ensure that they don't get ignored by the product owner simply because they might be "uninteresting to the customer" (Kniberg 2011). By factoring them into a functional story, they certainly can't be ignored, and the product owner will start to gain an appreciation for some of the technical complexity inherent within stories.

Addressing the second question, how to represent technical stories using the typical user story format, my answer is that you don't have to. I like the user story format for functional stories, but for technical stories, I find that the format isn't necessarily fit for purpose. Instead, simply use any format that makes sense and is easily communicated. Ensure that you set a consistent format that is as workable as possible for these technical types of stories. This same advice applies to capturing bugs in the product backlog. Although it is possible to document bugs utilizing the user story format, again, I find that taking this approach can become a bit contrived and confusing (like knocking a square peg into a round hole).

Consistency Is King

At the end of the day, the format you choose and how you break up your stories into tasks is totally up to you (incidentally, some teams don't even go down to this level). Scrum makes no mention of any of these details, so there are no prescribed rules to follow.

However, if you are to implement just one de facto rule, it should be that you are consistent with whatever approach you choose to take. That doesn't mean you are stuck with the same approach forever. As good Scrum practitioners, you no doubt will be constantly inspecting and adapting your processes. But once you have decided to give a particular approach a try, ensure that your team understands it and that it is maintained across all user requirements. This consistency creates a sense of discipline and is your insurance policy for those (hopefully rare) occasions when the product owner is not available to continue the conversation.

Shortcut 11: Developing the Definition of Done

I recently conquered what I consider to be one of my toughest Scrum challenges, and it's got nothing to do with my career. I finally convinced my completely non-techie wife, Carmen, to adopt "household Scrum"! We were finding that household tasks were simply not getting done at a sufficient rate ever since our daughter, Amy, made her entrance into the world. So I took my opportunity when it presented itself, and now our home is beautifully decorated with some eclectic sticky-note artwork!

Admittedly, I am not a great handyman, but I nonetheless completed one of my household Scrum tasks (fixing up a desk), and very proud of myself, I slapped the corresponding sticky-note into the Done column right in front of Carmen—oh yeah! Without skipping a beat, Carmen took the same sticky-note and placed it just as fervently back into the In Progress column with the accompanying commentary: "Umm, nice work fixing the desk, but that task has certainly not met *my* definition of done—your tools are still lying on the desk." Not only was I super-proud (because my wife had obviously been listening to my constant Scrum babbling), but also it reinforced an important lesson. The most important thing, when you have two or more humans involved in any type of transaction, is the setting and aligning of expectations. Scrum understands the criticality of this maxim and offers a vital construct to help us do so: the DoD (definition of done).

Ambiguous Arguments

Although debates centered on subjective topics can be fun, I usually find they are a big fat waste of time, especially in the workplace. You often go round and round in circles with no conclusive outcome and with all parties storming away frustrated or even resentful. I can't tell you the number of times I witnessed this type of argument in the "old days" between a programmer and a tester discussing quality. The programmers would vehemently argue that their code was perfectly fine for production, whereas the testers, tearing their hair out, would argue exactly opposite. So who was right? Well, both and neither. The problem was that the rules around what constituted a sufficient level of quality had not been clearly defined and/or had not been well communicated.

The DoD, if developed collaboratively, prevents such arguments from happening with any regularity (see Figure 4.2). The DoD becomes the governing agreement that guides all developmental activities, clearly stating what is required for a piece of work to be categorically classified as "done."

Where to Start

The first thing to realize when formulating your first DoD is that it isn't cast in stone. You don't need to spend an eternity deliberating what it should be, because it can evolve over time. Like everything else, we should be regularly inspecting and adapting the DoD. As Clinton Keith writes in *Agile Game Development with Scrum* (2010), "Teams expand the standard DoD by improving their practices. This enables the team to continually improve their effectiveness."

To compile an initial DoD, I recommend that you start extremely realistically or perhaps even conservatively. There is no definitive DoD that you can simply look up online. Your definition should be completely customized to take into account your product's specific requirements and your team's abilities and expectations (and

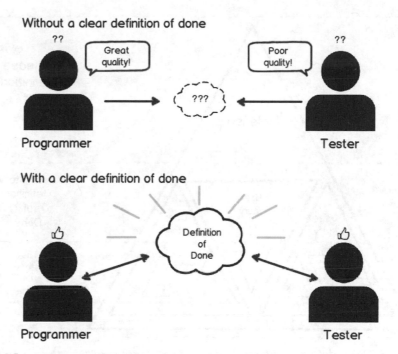

FIGURE 4.2   Aligning expectations with a clear definition of done minimizes
ambiguous arguments.

remember that these will certainly change over time). Also, ensure that the entire
Scrum team, including the developers, product owner, and ScrumMaster, is involved
in shaping the DoD.

Multiple Levels

The DoD can apply at several different levels. Tasks, user stories (see Shortcut 10),
and releases can all have a corresponding DoD (see Figure 4.3).

Let's look at some examples. Remember that there is no universal DoD; however,
here are some indicative definitions that I have worked with that may prove useful in
prompting discussion within your teams.

Task Level (Programming Task Example)

Task-level elements of the DoD include the following:

- Code has been unit tested.

- Code has been peer reviewed (if continual pair programming isn't being conducted) to ensure coding standards are met.

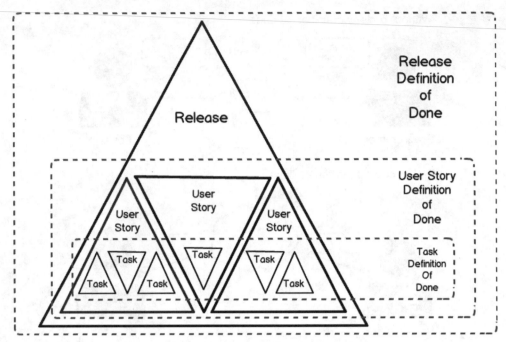

FIGURE 4.3   Your definition of done may have different levels.

- Code has been checked into source control with clear check-in comments for traceability.
- Checked-in code doesn't break the build (see Shortcut 18).
- The task board has been updated and remaining time for the task = 0 (see Shortcut 21).

User Story Level

There are two parts to this particular story (pardon the pun). The first part includes getting the actual user story requirements to a state of done to ensure that it is sprint-ready (sometimes called the *definition of ready*). The second (and more obvious) part is the DoD for determining when the story is ready for production release.

- **Definition of ready (see Figure 4.4)**
  - The user story has been estimated (see Shortcut 14).
  - There is a clearly defined set of acceptance criteria.
  - The user story has been uniquely ordered within the product backlog.

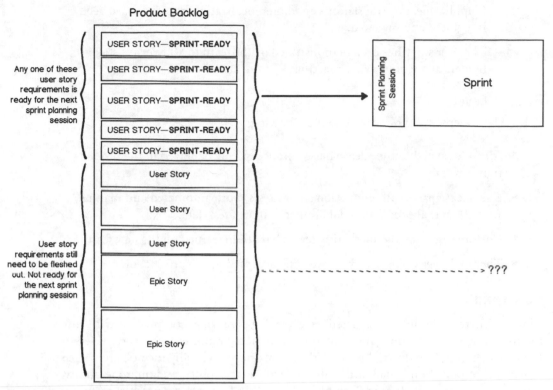

FIGURE 4.4   When a user story is sprint-ready, it can be moved into sprint planning.

- An appropriate and applicable level of extended documentation exists (such as mock-ups and wireframes if they are necessary).

- Based on the initial estimate, it should appear that the user story will comfortably fit within a single sprint

■ **Definition of done**

- All automated functional acceptance tests confirm that the new feature works as expected from end to end.

- All regression tests verify successful integration with other functions.

- Any relevant build/deploy scripts have been modified and tested.

- The final working functionality has been reviewed and accepted by the product owner.

- All relevant end-user documentation has been written and reviewed.

- If applicable, any translations and other localization elements have been integrated and reviewed.

- The user story has been demonstrated by the team to all relevant stakeholders at a sprint review meeting.

Release Level

Release level elements of done include the following:

- All code related to the release has been successfully deployed to the production servers.

- The release passes all production smoke tests (both automated and manual) with the actual production data rather than just test data.

- Customer service and marketing teams have been trained on the new features.

- The final release has been reviewed and accepted by the product owner.

Constraints

Along with the examples just listed, it often happens that compliance with any required system constraints (also called non-functional requirements) is reflected in the DoD. Often referred to as "-ilities," these constraints typically include areas such as scalability, portability, maintainability, security, extensibility, and interoperability. These are requirements that need to be baked into all layers of the product from the task level to the release level.

Here are some examples of these constraints:

- **Scalability:** Must be able to scale to 20,000 concurrent users.

- **Portability:** Any third-party technology used must be cross-platform.

- **Maintainability:** Clear modular design should be maintained across all components.

- **Security:** Must be able to hold up against specific security penetration tests.

- **Extensibility:** Must ensure that the data access layer can connect to all major commercial relational databases.

- **Interoperability:** Must be capable of data synchronization with all products in the same suite.

Acceptance Criteria or DoD?

Once your team becomes familiar with the DoD and the user story format, you will likely encounter an interesting question from time to time: Should XYZ requirement form part of the acceptance criteria or a part of the DoD? The answer to this question comes down to whether the requirement is applicable to every user story or to a smaller subset of stories. For example, let's look at backwards compatibility. If every feature of the product that is being developed must be completely backwards compatible with the previous version, then this nonfunctional requirement should form a part of the DoD. On the other hand, if it has been determined that backwards compatibility is necessary for only a handful of the features under development, then this requirement should be added to the list of acceptance criteria for just those features.

It's Just Like Cooking!

Similar to our discussion on defining DoD requirements (see Shortcut 10), the most important thing to remember is to remain consistent. Your DoD will evolve over time as requirements and abilities change. Starting with a detailed, overly ambitious list may look impressive at the onset, but as soon as it becomes unrealistic to adhere to, the team's credibility and morale will quickly dissipate. So, be realistic and get the ball rolling with a minimally acceptable DoD that everyone can live with—remember that it can evolve as the team matures.

It's like adding salt to your cooking—you can always add more, but it is much more difficult to remove once you've put in too much.

Shortcut 12: Progressive Revelations

As we age, certain parts of our body slowly start to change: the odd wrinkle here, an extra love handle there, and so on, and so forth. Luckily for those of us who aren't yet willing to age gracefully, there is a powerful tool that we can use every day to combat this transformation—it is that marvelous piece of reflective glass called the mirror! By looking at our reflection every day, we can inspect and quickly adapt to any slight deviation (if we choose to, of course). A new wrinkle—no problem, on goes some extra face cream; an extra bulge beginning to form—all good, an extra hard gym session should sort that one out!

Now imagine if you didn't look in the mirror for a year; there would be two likely outcomes. First, no doubt, you would be somewhat surprised by the (relatively) unfamiliar image looking back at you. Second, any perceived "degradation" would have compounded over the year, causing the "fix-up" work to be extensive, difficult to apply, and perhaps beyond remedy at this stage (contrary to what the cosmetics industry will tell you!).

Agile Coach Mike Dwyer (2010) poignantly blogs that "Scrum is not a silver bullet, Scrum is a silver mirror!" I find this statement to be helpful to illustrate that Scrum is not a silver bullet to resolve a project's woes but a silver mirror to help identify improvement areas earlier rather than later. In the past, waterfallers wouldn't look closely at the product or process under development until right at the end. Scrum gives teams the opportunity to frequently look in the mirror to discover the early-stage wrinkles, which allows the team to take action before the problems grow worse.

You may be thinking that this is a shortcut dedicated to the important sprint retrospective or sprint review sessions, but it actually isn't. Instead, it focuses on a more informal intra-sprint activity that many teams call a *walkthrough*. The purpose of a walkthrough is to inspect and adapt the user stories under development on a day-to-day basis throughout the sprint. *So what about the sprint review?* I hear you ask. While sprint reviews are indeed a regular opportunity to look in the mirror, conducting even more frequent checks can help eliminate additional waste by closing the feedback loop faster while also providing the opportunity to engage in continuous deployment/delivery (see Shortcut 18). I still believe the sprint review has considerable value, but I see it more as an opportunity to present and discuss the output of the sprint with a broader section of the stakeholder community (see Shortcut 22).

Verification and Validation

The purpose of a walkthrough is to reassure the team that the work undertaken (or about to be undertaken) is going to deliver what everyone is expecting. A walkthrough may be requested by a developer wishing to verify with the product owner that he or she hasn't misinterpreted the objective of the work they are about to launch into. Alternatively, the product owner may wish to call for a walkthrough with a developer to verify design decisions before too much time and energy is invested.

How many times have you been involved in a waterfall project where the product manager (using the old vernacular), with wide, startled eyes, exclaims at the end of development, "This isn't what I meant! I thought it would function like blah, blah!" This would elicit a gruff response from the developers along the lines of "Then why on page 47 of version 3.6.4 of the specification document, which has been signed off by half the company, does it clearly state otherwise?!"

I'm not saying that breakdowns in communication will cease to exist with Scrum, and in fact, with the emphasis on increasing the frequency of face-to-face discussions, you may well find that there are more disagreements. However, the key here is that the more regular the interaction, the easier it will be to smooth out any contention and get everyone pulling in the same direction again.

When, Where, Who

A walkthrough should occur whenever it is needed. Some teams that I have worked with prefer to allocate a couple of periods in the day (typically an hour following the daily scrum and another hour midafternoon). This practice doesn't necessarily require that all team members attend walkthroughs for 2 hours a day, but it sets an expectation that they *may* be interrupted during these times, so they should not get frustrated if they get a tap on the shoulder from someone requesting a walkthrough.

Because the walkthrough is typically a hands-on demonstration of the work requiring verification/validation, it usually occurs at the desk of the applicable developer. There is no need to get tied down with red tape by sending out meeting requests and booking rooms for a walkthrough. However, if you don't have the luxury of a collocated development team, you obviously need to consider some additional logistics.

In relation to who should attend a walkthrough, I recommend that you try to always include the product owner, the relevant programmer(s), and the relevant tester(s) at the same time. With more reliance on discussion than on specification, it is important to ensure that everyone is on the same page (ironic choice of phrase, I know) at the same time.

Issues and Adjustments

A walkthrough should be purely focused on the current sprint backlog items rather than providing a forum to discuss future stories—leave that for your sprint planning session (see Shortcut 8). Valid outputs from a walkthrough typically fall into three categories:

- **Issues:** These are problems during development that manifest in broken functionality that needs fixing (see Shortcut 9).

- **Adjustments:** Consider adjustments to be minor changes to the design, not to be confused with wholesale scope creep to the user story.

- **Thumbs up and smiling faces:** That's what you get if the walkthrough verifies that the work in progress is on the money!

Be Aware of Scope Creep

What happens if the product owner, after having a "taste test" during a walkthrough, decides that he or she wants to adjust the "flavor" (and I'm not just talking about a pinch of salt). This can be a common and potentially frustrating situation, but it is not a problem if handled correctly.

Remember from Shortcut 1 that once the scope of the sprint is set, it should be left alone and protected to provide the developers with some reassurance that their focus can remain intact for the duration of the sprint. Although minor adjustments should be accepted and expected, significantly changing the requirements for a user story mid-sprint must be avoided (see Figure 4.5). So what should happen if this situation arises? As an example, let's say the product owner decides that the shopping cart requires more than the previously agreed upon number of payment options. No problem. Simply create an additional user story that focuses purely on the new payment options, and add it to the product backlog. If this is considered to be of high priority, then present it in the next sprint planning session and tackle it in the subsequent sprint rather than changing the scope of the current one.

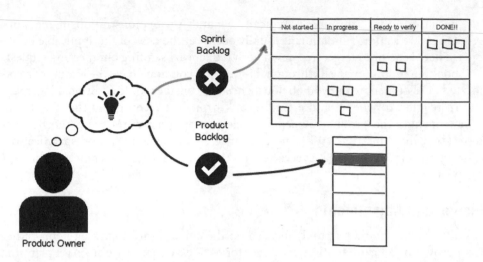

FIGURE 4.5   Minor adjustments can be accommodated, but save the big changes for the product backlog and future sprints.

Capturing the Output

Although teams should be encouraged to resolve issues and adjustments in real time during the walkthrough (if the change is relatively trivial), there are times when it isn't possible to do so. In such situations, it is important that the issues are not forgotten when the time comes to tidy things up. I recommend the following simple approach to ensure that you're not wasting too much time in documentation mode.

1. Add a dotted line under the current list of acceptance criteria for the user story to distinguish the new notes from the original requirements.

2. Add the initials of the walkthrough attendees as well as a date and time stamp to help the team more easily recall when the modifications were discussed should memories become hazy.

3. Define the requirements with short, sharp bullet points (see Figure 4.6).

4. New changes are likely to spawn some new tasks, extend the length of existing tasks, or both. That's fine, but make sure the time remaining for existing tasks is adjusted accordingly. I also recommend adding new tasks to the task board using sticky-notes in a different color than used for the original tasks (see Shortcut 21).

Don't Overdo It

In Brisbane, where I grew up, there is a set of outdoor climbing cliffs in the heart of the city where city-dwellers can escape to enjoy some face time with nature. Although

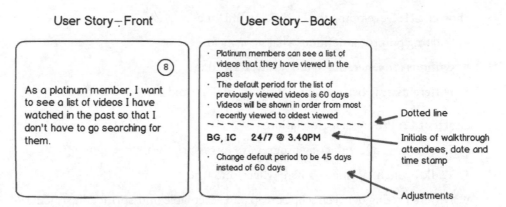

FIGURE 4.6   An example of how minor adjustments can be captured on the back of the user story card.

climbing isn't necessarily my sport of choice, I would occasionally venture down to admire the nerve and flexibility of these human spiders. I recall the particularly courageous (aka crazy) climbers who would free-climb—that is, climb without using support ropes from the top but instead incrementally anchor themselves in as they progressed. The further apart these anchors are, the higher the risk and the longer the recovery time should a slip occur. However, climbers who obsessively and too frequently create anchors inevitably end up wasting energy and time as well as losing the valuable rhythm and focus required to reach the top.

The intra-sprint walkthrough is analogous to free-climb anchoring in that walkthroughs should occur as frequently as necessary to ensure "safety," but they should not be conducted just for the sake of it—you don't want to unnecessarily spend the team's precious time and energy.

Wrap Up

The three shortcuts in this chapter focused on a selection of tactics, tools, and tips to help your team define and evolve their requirements and definition of done. Let's recap what was covered:

Shortcut 10: Structuring Stories

- An overview of the user story hierarchy

- Approaches for breaking down sprint-ready user stories into tasks

- Options for incorporating technical requirements into the sprint backlog

Shortcut 11: Developing the Definition of Done

- Starting points for defining what *done* means
- Options for generating multiple levels of done
- Differentiating between the definition of done and acceptance criteria

Shortcut 12: Progressive Revelations

- The benefits of conducting progressive intra-sprint walkthroughs
- Walkthrough logistics—when, where, and who
- Differentiating between scope creep and acceptable mid-sprint adjustments

Chapter 5
ESTABLISHING ESTIMATES

Like it or not, the need to provide estimates for software projects isn't going to disappear. Thankfully, the typical estimation burden that afflicts many teams can become significantly reduced should they choose to adopt the de facto standard for estimating Scrum projects: *relative estimation.*

The following three shortcuts introduce you to the concept of relative estimation and provide guidance on how to transition from traditional time-based estimation.

Shortcut 13: Relating to Estimating introduces the elegance of the relative estimation approach. Shortcut 14: Planning Poker at Pace provides a range of tips and tricks to ensure efficient Planning Poker sessions. Finally, Shortcut 15: Transitioning Relatively offers advice to assist teams in transitioning from time-based estimation to relative estimation.

Shortcut 13: Relating to Estimating

Like many of you reading this shortcut, I have spent an inordinate number of hours watching time whittle away during long-winded estimation sessions in the quest to meticulously break down nebulous requirements into detailed tasks (on very long and very stripy Gantt charts). But worse than the time wasted actually creating these Gantt charts was the significant time spent reworking them on almost a daily basis as the inevitable changes to scope—not to mention adjustments to estimates—flooded in.

It wasn't long before I realized that the only good to come out of this situation was that we now had some interesting-looking stripy wallpaper to decorate the office with!

And thus began my epic quest to find a more effective approach to help conquer the dark art of estimation. After much searching, I stumbled across what I consider to be the most effective technique for estimating emergent requirements: relative estimation. The elegant simplicity of this new approach finally convinced me that there was in fact some light at the end of the long, dark estimation tunnel.

Estimation Pain

Before jumping into the ins and outs of relative estimation, let's go right back to basics and consider why estimation is so hard and painful (especially in our software world).

First, we humans are not naturally great estimators. We tend to either be optimists or pessimists and very rarely realists. I don't even need to back this assertion up with statistics because I am confident that anyone reading this paragraph will agree!

In addition, especially in the world of software, there are numerous unknowns: technology constantly changes and requirements are emergent. There are many moving parts as well as intricate dependencies between tasks (and between people), and that's not even throwing in external environmental factors!

Why Bother Estimating?

If our estimates carry such a significant chance of being inaccurate, then why bother estimating at all? Well, I believe that even if our estimates aren't always correct, there are still very important reasons to estimate, and I'm going to talk about two of them.

The first reason is to help us make trade-off decisions. For example, let's say that I were to ask a couple living in San Francisco whether they would prefer a vacation to Australia or a vacation to Mexico—which one would they choose? Sure, they might have a preference for one or the other, but two other big factors come into play—time and budget. While they might prefer a trip to Australia, let's say (yes, I'm a little biased), they might not have enough accrued leave (time) to justify the long trip or enough budget (as the Aussie dollar is pretty strong at time of writing!). So how do they calculate whether they can afford to take this particular trip? Well, they simply estimate how long the trip might take and how much the trip might cost. The same principle applies to requirements that make up the wish-lists for our software products.

The second reason is to help set goals. If you're anything like me, when you set a deadline for yourself, you do everything in your power to make sure you hit it. Sure, there will be times when your estimates are way off—and it shouldn't necessitate unsustainable heroics—but the act of estimating and setting targets can certainly help you to maintain focus and maximize results.

Now that you're convinced that estimation is a worthwhile exercise, we can dive right into the details of relative estimation.

Explaining Relative Estimation

Relative estimation is applied at a product backlog level rather than at a sprint backlog level. Sprint backlog items can be estimated in traditional time units (such as hours) primarily because the period of time being estimated for is a single sprint (typically a matter of days rather than months) and the requirements will be defined in enough detail. On the other hand, product backlog items (PBIs) are more loosely defined and may collectively represent many months of work, making time-based estimation very difficult, if not impossible.

Relative estimation applies the principle that *comparing* is much quicker and more accurate than *deconstructing*. That is, instead of trying to break down a requirement into constituent tasks (and estimating these tasks), teams compare the relative effort of completing a new requirement to the relative effort of a previously estimated requirement. I'll use an analogy to demonstrate what I mean.

The Stair Climber

Let's say we have four buildings. Three of them are modern, while the other is older and somewhat decrepit. They are all different sizes. We are asked to estimate how long it will take us in total to walk to the top floor of all the buildings using the stairs (see Figure 5.1).

Having never completed an exercise like this, we have some unknowns to consider. For example, we are not sure how physically fit we are or what types of obstacles we might need to negotiate in the stairwells.

So, what do we do? Well, we could take the time to count every floor of every building and then estimate how long it might take us to go up the counted flights of stairs despite not knowing our fitness or the state of the stairwells. This estimate not only will take considerable time but also will be grossly inaccurate if our assumptions are way off the mark.

Let's explore another option. First, let's classify the buildings into what we'll call "effort classes," with the smallest building considered a 10-point class. The choice of 10 is arbitrary—it could have been 100, 1,000, or any number for that matter (you'll soon see why it makes no difference). We take a look at building 2, and we think it looks about three times the size of our 10-point building; therefore, we classify it as a

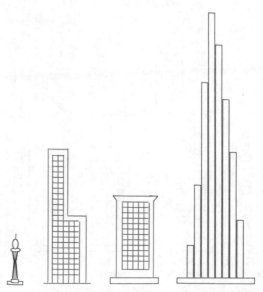

FIGURE 5.1 How do we estimate how long it will take us to walk up all of these buildings using the stairs?

30-point class. Our third building (the older one) is somewhere in the middle, so we would typically call it a 20-pointer, but because of its aging state, there may be more risks and impediments getting up the stairwell, so we take these factors into account and give it a point value of 25. Our final massive building is about twice the size of our second building (the 30-pointer), so it becomes a 60-point class building (see Figure 5.2).

Note that these points are simply relative markers to help us compare. The numbers do not relate to a specific unit of size or time—they are just classification markers.

This little exercise allows us to quickly estimate the effort of our four climbs—not in absolute terms but in relative terms. This information forms the first piece of the puzzle. We might now have an idea of the relative effort of climbing one building compared to another, but we still need to work out an estimate for the duration of the overall exercise.

What next? Well, how about we first invest a little time to actually test our fitness and check the state of an indicative stairwell? Let's time-box this experiment to 10 minutes (our nominated sprint duration) and see how far we manage to get (see Figure 5.3).

To the stairwell we go and, after 10 minutes, we find ourselves halfway up building 1 (the 10-point building). With this information, we can work out what our

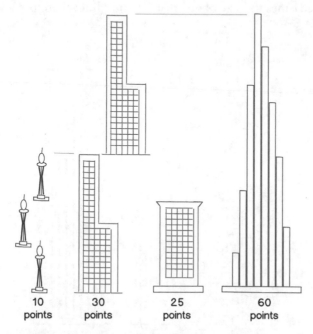

| 10 points | 30 points | 25 points | 60 points |

FIGURE 5.2   We can classify our buildings in relative terms by making some quick comparisons.

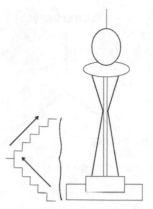

FIGURE 5.3   After 10 minutes of actual stair climbing, we get halfway up the 10-point building.

velocity is, or, in other words, the amount of work (in points) that we are able to achieve within our 10-minute sprint. Based on the fact that we climbed halfway up the 10-point building, we can say that our velocity is 5 points per sprint, or more succinctly, 5 points.

"But we need to know how long it will take us to reach the top of all four buildings," I hear you say? Well, how about some simple extrapolation. Let's start by totaling the amount of work to do by adding up the relative sizes of the buildings: 10 + 30 + 25 + 60 = 125 points.

We then take our velocity (remember, it was 5 points) and, using some simple math, we divide the total 125 points by our 5-point velocity to give us 25 sprints. We know that each sprint is worth 10 minutes, so we have 250 minutes so far. We can then add another 50 minutes (20 percent of our estimated time) for some extra buffer (for catching our breath and for elevator rides back down), and voilá, we can give a rough estimate of 300 minutes, or 6 hours, to complete our exercise!

Software Relative Estimation

Let's apply this new concept to our software projects. Instead of estimating our stair-climbing prowess, we need to estimate the effort required to complete PBIs.

First, we should determine the effort required to complete a PBI using three factors: complexity, repetition, and risk (see Figure 5.4).

Let me explain the difference: we may have a PBI that requires the design of a *complex* optimization algorithm. It may not require many lines of code but instead a lot of thinking and analysis time.

Next, we may have a PBI that is user-interface focused, requiring significant HTML tweaking across multiple browser types and versions. Although this work is not complex per se, it is very *repetitious*, requiring a lot of trial and error.

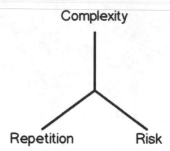

FIGURE 5.4   The three factors that determine how much effort is required to complete a PBI.

Another PBI might require interfacing with a new third-party product that we haven't dealt with before. This is a requirement with *risk* and may require significant time to overcome teething issues.

When sizing up a PBI, it is necessary to take all of these factors into account.

Another point to note is that we don't require detailed specifications to make effort estimates. If the product owner wants a login screen, we don't need to know what the exact mechanics, workflow, screen layouts, and so on, are going to be. Those can come later when we actually implement the requirement within a sprint. All we need to know at this early stage is roughly how much effort the login function is going to require relative to, let's say, a search requirement that we had already estimated. We could say that if the search function was allocated 20 points, then the login function should be allocated 5 points on the assumption that it will require approximately a quarter the effort.

Velocity

We discussed the core purpose of the velocity metric, but there are a few other important factors to be aware of:

- Velocity is calculated by summing up the points of all PBIs completed in a sprint.

- The most common approach for handling partially completed PBIs is to award points only to the sprint in which the PBI actually met its definition of done (see Shortcut 11).

- Although a velocity can certainly be generated with only one sprint, the reality is that it won't necessarily reflect the longer-term average because velocity tends to fluctuate from sprint to sprint. This fluctuation can happen for a number of reasons, including the impact of partially completed stories, the impact of impediments, and team member availability (or lack thereof), to name just a few. Using an average velocity or rolling average of the last three sprints is a simple option for calculating a more indicative velocity. For an even more comprehensive and accurate calculation of velocity, I recommend you use Cohn's free velocity range calculator,[1] but note that to use this tool, you need to have data from at least five sprints.

- Velocity is reliant on maintaining the same team makeup and the same sprint length—otherwise, calculating velocity is much harder.

Relative Estimation in Practice

To put relative estimation into practice, many teams play a nifty game called Planning Poker. Shortcut 14 explains the mechanics of this effective technique and offers a selection of tips and tricks to make it as effective and efficient as possible.

Speaking of practice, it is important to understand and accept that estimation is hard. Very hard. Software development is burdened with high levels of complexity (and many unknowns), yet it requires perfection for the software to compile and work. Because of these factors, no estimation approach is going to be foolproof. However, I truly believe that relative story point estimation is, at the very least, just as accurate as any alternative while offering the advantage of being far more simple and elegant in comparison.

Shortcut 14: Planning Poker at Pace

With relative story point estimation now in your arsenal, you finally have a weapon to wield in the battle against the forces that make software estimation so painful. Relative estimation is simple, makes sense, and is way more fun than other long-winded and misleading estimation techniques!

The technique we use to conduct relative estimation is a game invented by James Grenning and popularized by Mike Cohn called *Planning Poker*. It is based on a method developed in the 1970s called Wideband Delphi that evolved from an earlier version (Delphi) invented in the 1950s by the RAND Corporation. This approach utilizes broad insight from a group of cross-functional experts to arrive at an estimate that is typically more accurate than one derived from a single person.

Setting Up the Game

The technique is called Planning Poker because teams literally play with cards. But, instead of spades, hearts, clubs, and diamonds, they use cards representing story point values. A common point system that is utilized for these values is Mike Cohn's modified Fibonacci sequence:

$$\frac{1}{2}, 1, 2, 3, 5, 8, 13, 20, 40, 100, \infty \text{ (infinity)}$$

---

1. Mike Cohn's free velocity calculator can be found at www.mountaingoatsoftware.com/tools/velocity-range-calculator.

In case you were wondering, I believe a fair translation for the infinity card would be something along the lines of, "Whoa! That is way too big to estimate—it definitely needs splitting before any meaningful estimation can occur."

I'm a fan of using the modified Fibonacci sequence because it helps to reflect the greater amount of uncertainty that exists as requirements get larger (see Figure 5.5) while also avoiding the perception of precision (hence the change from 21 to 20, 42 to 40 and so on). That being said, it does come with a potential problem especially with new teams. If you recall from Shortcut 14, the point values should not correlate to a specific time or distance unit. The issue when using Fibonacci numbers is that people can get into the bad habit of equating 13 points to 13 hours, for example.

To combat this situation, some teams adopt more abstract classifiers, such as T-shirt sizes:

XS, S, M, L, XL, XXL

I personally don't use this extra layer of abstraction because it requires the extra step of mapping to a numeric value to enable forecasting during release planning— remember how in Shortcut 13 we calculated the time it would take to climb the buildings by dividing by the numeric velocity value?

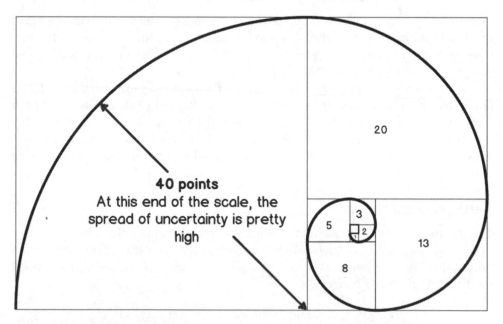

FIGURE 5.5   The modified Fibonacci sequence is an approximation of the logarithmic "golden spiral" where greater uncertainty exists as requirements get larger.

Planning Poker Mechanics

Before we proceed with some Planning Poker hints and tips to ensure that your sessions don't become late-night marathons, let's run through a brief overview of the mechanics of the game.

The session proceeds as follows:

1. The product owner describes the top PBI before the team is invited to ask questions to clarify the scope and desired benefits. Any changes to the PBI description or acceptance criteria are captured progressively.

2. Once ready to estimate, each team member places, facedown on the table, the card he or she feels best represents the effort required to complete the PBI.

3. Once they have chosen their cards, all team members simultaneously flip their cards face up.

4. When there is a lack of agreement, the holder of the high card has a short debate (a few minutes at most) with the low-card representative under close observation from the rest of the team.

5. With the new evidence uncovered during the debate, the team returns to step 2.

6. Steps 2 through 5 are repeated until a general consensus is reached for the PBI.

7. Once the PBI has been assigned a value, the process starts again from step 1 for the next PBI in the product backlog (see Figure 5.6).

Note that the ScrumMaster acts as the facilitator throughout and is not involved in the actual estimation.

A key requirement is that everyone must estimate the effort for the entire PBI as opposed to just estimating the bit that pertains to his or her specialty. For example, a programmer needs to estimate the effort of not just the coding work but also the testing and deployment work—an interesting concept, right?

So, how does everyone participate in estimates of work that is not in their primary area of expertise? Well, they need to base the combined estimate on experience. Even though they might not have done much of the testing, they will remember what was involved when a similar PBI was implemented in the past. They will recall, for example, that even though the programming wasn't too tricky, the testing was a nightmare because of the various integration points with the third-party payment system they were using. It is common for individuals to assume that they are estimating only for their specific function, and it is a common reason that new teams typically start with very disparate estimates (so beware of this pitfall).

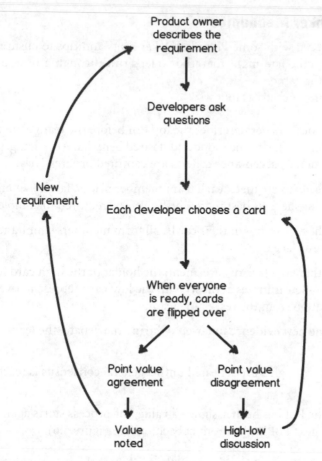

FIGURE 5.6   The flow of a typical Planning Poker cycle.

When to Play Planning Poker

The first Planning Poker session should take place after the initial product backlog is compiled, and subsequent games can be played whenever a new PBI is added to the backlog or in the rare situation that reestimation is called for. Reestimation should be required only when a whole class of PBIs suddenly becomes smaller or larger (relatively speaking). When does this situation occur? Let's say that a set of your PBIs rely on integration with a third party. Their API has been flimsy, at best, and you know that workarounds, not to mention a whole heap of extra testing, will need to be applied. Let's say they finally release a brand-new, super-improved interface that removes the need for workarounds and additional testing—all of a sudden, any PBIs reliant on it become relatively smaller.

Get the Team Warmed Up

To get the entire team ready for a Planning Poker session, it's important to circulate a small number of reference PBIs that correspond to the point levels in the card deck (see Shortcut 15).

This process calibrates everybody's yardsticks nice and early so that the team will be able to immediately recall what a 13-point PBI is and what a 1-point PBI is (as well as everything in between). Send these references out a few days before the session, followed by a quick reminder on the morning of the session.

Big Cards for Big Occasions

I typically advocate removing the big cards (20, 40, 100, infinity) as well as the ½ card from the Planning Poker deck. The rationale behind this decision is that you effectively cut the total choice of cards down to six, and fewer options equals less analysis paralysis. Further, it discourages product owners from bringing to the table any stories that are too large and nebulous.

That being said, Mike Cohn (2011) raises a valid scenario in which the big cards will come in handy:

> Suppose your boss wants to know the general size of a new project being considered. The boss doesn't need a perfect, very precise estimate. Something like "around a year" or "three to six months" is enough in this case. To answer this question you'll want to write a product backlog. You want to put no more effort into this than you need to. Since the boss wants a high-level estimate, you can write a high-level product backlog. Big user story "epics" that describe large swaths of functionality will suffice. . . . And these epic user stories can be estimated with the large story point values.

If nothing else, using these big numbers will indicate to all involved that there is a high level of uncertainty and that the best estimate that can be offered at this early stage is one of general magnitude rather than specific duration.

Don't Double Up

As often happens, a group of PBIs will inevitably rely on some of the same important research or technical plumbing. If this is the case, ensure that the same work is not estimated multiple times. This underlying work should be incorporated into the estimation of only one of the PBIs, not into all of them. Which PBI you decide to incorporate these extra tasks into is up to you, but try to select the one you anticipate will be implemented first. Although this advice might sound obvious, you may find that your team assumes they are estimating PBIs in isolation unless you make this point explicitly clear.

Reaching a Consensus

After some discussion, the team will play its first round of Planning Poker. If it doesn't result in consensus, I recommend asking the following questions:

- Have you considered *all* the necessary functions and not just individual specializations?

- Do you have a hard or soft opinion about that score? If it is soft, are you comfortable switching your value?

- Is anyone on the borderline between two values? If so, are you comfortable moving to the more popular adjacent score?

If there is no consensus after asking these questions, it is time to facilitate a quick debate between a representative of the high card and a representative of the low card. The trick here is to make sure the debate doesn't become a drawn-out, granular technical discussion. The simple message to the debaters is to base their arguments on the relative comparison of the PBI being estimated to the reference PBIs (rather than on the complexities of the potential technical implementation). Remember from Shortcut 13 that relative estimation focuses on comparing rather than deconstructing.

Finally, if the team simply cannot reach an agreement between two adjacent values, you should err on the side of caution and use the higher value.

Phones Can Help

Unless you're a hard-core disciplinarian, you will find people occasionally checking their phones for messages. If they're playing Angry Birds,[2] then you've got bigger problems! Instead of being the scolding teacher, make their devices part of the session. Get the team to download one of the legitimate, licensed Planning Poker apps and use their devices instead of the traditional cards. Not only does playing Planning Poker on a phone make it more difficult to play around with Angry Birds, it also saves you from that laborious task of sorting through the cards at the end of the session!

It's All about Benefits

After you've played some Planning Poker and used the advice from this shortcut, the estimation benefits should be obvious. But what happens when your boss calls you into his office to discuss concerns about the team playing card games on the company's dollar? Well, here are some extra benefits you can explain to transform him into a Planning Poker advocate:

---

2. To learn more about Angry Birds, go to http://en.wikipedia.org/wiki/Angry_Birds.

- The ability to rapidly estimate long-term product backlogs without requiring detailed specifications and complicated dependency mapping.

- The ability to provide broader insight from a diverse set of functional experts to ensure that estimates aren't being padded or underbaked.

- The ability to leverage the knowledge obtained from completing legacy work.

- The ability for the team to actually have some fun while conducting a traditionally mundane and frustrating task. Planning Poker sessions are interactive, lively, and much faster than traditional estimation marathons!

Remember Parkinson's Law

Speaking from experience, if the ScrumMaster doesn't control the pace and focus of Planning Poker sessions, they will become endless talkfests or could even turn into pitched battle (personally, I don't know which one is worse!).

Time-box your discussions and always remember Parkinson's law: "Work expands so as to fill the time available for its completion" (Parkinson 1993).

I assure you that if you apply the suggestions given in this shortcut, your Planning Poker sessions will not only become punchier (as in faster, not more violent) but everyone will enjoy them a great deal more!

Shortcut 15: Transitioning Relatively

Hopefully, if you are reading this shortcut, it means that you're now convinced that relative estimation is a great way to move forward. The lights are dimmed, the sunglasses are on, and the cards are ready to be dealt for your inaugural Planning Poker session (see Shortcut 14). But hang on—where do you start? What does a 1-point user story actually mean? How about a 13-pointer? What is the best way to initially calibrate so that the team has a foundation to work from? If these are the questions that are running through your mind, then please read on.

An Approach

One calibration approach that some teams like to use is to identify the smallest user story in the product backlog and designate it to be the initial ½-point story (assuming they are using the Fibonacci sequence). Once this initial baseline has been confirmed, the team works its way down the list of user stories and allocates 1 point for any story that is roughly double the ½-pointer, 2 points for any story that is roughly double a 1-pointer, and so on.

This approach can certainly work, and it seems straightforward on the surface, but the reality is that it can end up taking considerably more time than you might expect. First, the team has to actually traverse through the entire product backlog to identify the starting contenders, and second, the team needs to reach a consensus as to which user story should become the actual initial baseline.

Bear in mind that your team is new to this process, so it helps to reduce as much ambiguity as possible. It is for this reason that I like to calibrate story points by utilizing work completed in the past.

Using Historical Work

The idea behind leveraging historical work is to help create mappings between known quantities (old completed work) and the new Fibonacci story point values (or whatever other scale you choose to use).

Using historical work offers a team two significant advantages: familiarity and consistency.

Familiarity

It is obvious that any team will be more familiar with work that they completed previously than with work they are going to do in the future. This familiarity proves to be particularly helpful when playing Planning Poker (see Shortcut 14) because instead of comparing future unknown work to other future unknown work (similar to the first approach described earlier), teams can compare future unknown work with past known work. Not only does this approach remove an element of ambiguity, but also, the speed at which these comparisons take place will be much quicker because the team can more readily recollect the historical work.

Consistency

When historical work forms the set of benchmarks (for the various point values in the Planning Poker deck), these same benchmarks can be used across any and all projects that the same team works on down the track. This early work will naturally speed up future proceedings because the initial benchmarking process is required only once (as opposed to whenever a new product backlog is formulated and presented).

Creating the Mappings

Five steps are required when creating the mappings between the historical work and the new point scale. Steps 2 and 3 in the following process are inspired by James Grenning's article "Planning Poker Party" (2009), which describes a similar approach (using a new product backlog rather than historical work).

Step 1: Identify

Identify a recent project that the same team (or at least most of the team) was involved in. List the discrete pieces of work, and write them on index cards (if they are in digital form). If they are not already in the user story format (see Shortcut 10), they should be converted to ensure comparative consistency moving forward (see Figure 5.7).

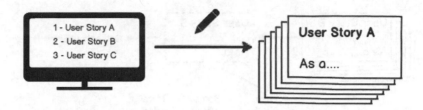

FIGURE 5.7 Transcribe any digital requirements onto index cards.

Step 2: Sort and Stack

For this next step, you need a nice, big table and the development team. Starting with the first index card, read the user story out loud and place it on the table (see Figure 5.8).

Next, take the second card and ask the team whether they recall it taking more, less, or the same amount of effort as the first card (see Figure 5.9). If it took less effort, place it to the left of the original; if it took more effort, place it to the right; and if it took roughly the same amount of effort, stack it on top of the first. If there is any contention or confusion, " burn" the card (not literally, please).

Then take the next card and place it either to the left of both cards (if it took less effort than both), to the right of both cards (if it took more effort than both), between the cards (if its effort was somewhere in the middle), or on top of one of the cards (if it was roughly the same effort). Repeat this process for all of the index cards (see Figure 5.10).

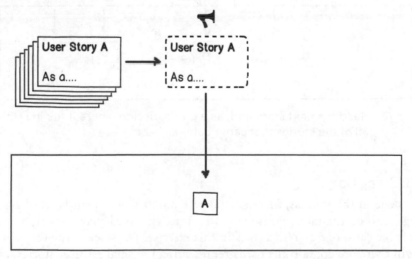

FIGURE 5.8 Read the first story out loud and place it on the table.

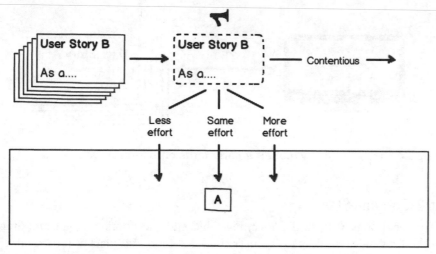

FIGURE 5.9   Read the second story and, as a group, decide whether it took more, less, or the same amount of effort as the first story.

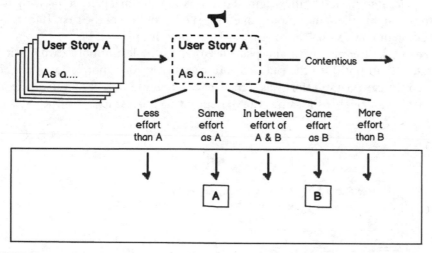

FIGURE 5.10   Read the next story and, as a group, decide where it fits in relation to all of the stories that came before it.

Step 3: Sizing Up

At this stage in the process, there should be a number of sequential card stacks (of varying sizes) on the table. Please note that I use the word *stack* loosely, as you can certainly have just one card in a stack in this exercise. The stack at the very left of the table will therefore contain the cards representing the smallest user stories, and the stack representing the largest stories will be located at the very right end of the table.

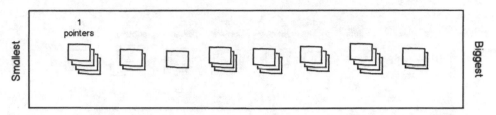

FIGURE 5.11   With all the sorting done, the smallest stories will be on one side of the table and the largest stories will be on the other.

Now, it's time to play some Planning Poker (see Shortcut 14). Automatically assign all cards in the leftmost stack a 1-point value (see Figure 5.11). As an aside, I like to reserve the smallest ½-point value for trivial changes, such as label adjustments or textbox alignments, so unless your smallest stack is made up of these tiny requirements, consider starting with 1 point rather than ½ point.

Starting with a representative from the second-smallest stack (directly to the right of your new 1-pointers), determine the relative effort that was required to complete it compared to a representative from the smallest stack (for example, it may be three times as much effort).

As each stack gets classified, place a card representing its relative point value above it for quick recollection, so using our example, the second stack would be tagged with a 3-pointer card.

Step 4: Subclassify

With any luck, your Planning Poker session ran smoothly (thanks to the tips that you picked up in Shortcut 14), leaving you with several stacks of user stories with corresponding point values.

In a perfect world, there will be a stack that corresponds to each value in the point system that you're using (see Figure 5.12), but do not worry if this isn't the case. At the end of the day, so long as you have a couple of benchmark stories, you can at least get started.

If you happen to be spoiled for choice by having stacks containing a number of stories, then you can further classify them into subcategories that relate to different

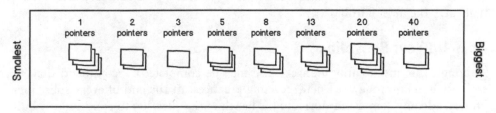

FIGURE 5.12   After playing Planning Poker and assigning values, you might have stacks that look like this.

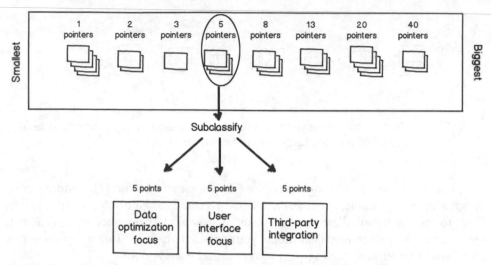

FIGURE 5.13   You can consider subclassifying stories in the same stack by their different focal points.

areas of focus (see Figure 5.13). For example, you could end up with three different 5-point stories. Even though they are grouped together (based on similar effort), they could all have very different focal points. Story 1 could have data optimization complexities, story 2 could have more of a user-interface focus, and story 3 could require integration with a third-party product. By subclassifying in this manner, the ability to compare apples to apples (when estimating new product backlogs) becomes a reality.

Step 5: Final Filter

The final step in this calibration exercise is to filter out one representative from each stack (or substack if you subclassified as explained in step 4). These final champions will become the reference stories that are used to help start off future Planning Poker sessions (on new product backlogs). Considering that the stories have already been classified, the selection of the reference stories can be based on choosing a random story from the stack, or if you wish to be more discerning, the team can select stories that carry the most familiarity.

Keep Up Your Recycling

Although the initial calibration exercise may be complete, I recommend that you embrace and continue your new recycling practices. At the end of every subsequent project, add any completed stories to the benchmark collection to continuously build up a rich library of stories that are not only familiar but also easily relatable to a variety of different requirements.

There you have it. You are now equipped with a process to leverage historical work to calibrate some relative benchmarks. By utilizing work completed in the past, the team gains the added benefits of familiarity and consistency, making the transition to relative estimation smoother and less ambiguous.

Wrap Up

The three shortcuts included in this chapter focused on a selection of tactics, tools, and tips to help your team understand and transition to the world of relative estimation. Let's recap what was covered:

Shortcut 13: Relating to Estimating

- Fundamental reasons for estimating requirements
- An explanation of relative estimation using some easy-to-understand metaphors
- Factors that influence a meaningful velocity

Shortcut 14: Planning Poker at Pace

- The mechanics of a Planning Poker session
- Tips to ensure that the team is warmed up and ready to launch into a game of Planning Poker
- Additional spinoff benefits that Planning Poker offers

Shortcut 15: Transitioning Relatively

- The benefits of using historical work to calibrate some initial reference points
- How to create mappings between legacy requirements and story points
- The process of generating a broad selection of meaningful reference points for future estimation sessions

Chapter 6

QUESTIONING QUALITY

It's no secret that compromised quality was a regular feature of traditional waterfall software projects, primarily due to the highly risky practice of all-in-one integration and testing at the very end. Although Scrum's focus on iterative and incremental development alleviates significant risk, the reality is that we will never be able to totally eliminate every defect.

The following three shortcuts step you through both preemptive measures and remedial actions to help deal with those pesky bugs.

Shortcut 16: Bah! Scrum Bug! lays out a selection of new definitions, principles, and processes to assist in managing defects during sprints. Shortcut 17: We Still Love the Testers! considers the new roles that a tester now plays on a Scrum team. Finally, Shortcut 18: Automation Nation identifies a selection of important starting points when commencing down the path of test automation.

Shortcut 16: Bah! Scrum Bug!

Although we no longer have to contend with actual moths infiltrating our vacuum tubes (yep, that's where the term *bug* originates), their digital descendants are still regular visitors to every codebase on the planet. In the same way that bugs have changed over time, so has the way that they are dealt with, and this is particularly pertinent to our new agile way of thinking.

Previously, our waterfalling world viewed the handling of bugs very sequentially (see Figure 6.1).

With this simplified process as the benchmark, let's look at what needs to change when implementing Scrum. In particular, it is important to appreciate that programming and testing need to be conducted in tandem rather than in sequential phases if teams hope to deliver working functionality early and often.

New Definitions

Before exploring some new Scrum-friendly processes for handling bugs, I'd like to set up some foundations with a few definitions and principles that I like to use.

Definition 1: Issues

- An *issue* is a problem that occurs during the sprint and is tightly coupled to a user story (see Shortcut 10) that has not yet met its definition of done (see

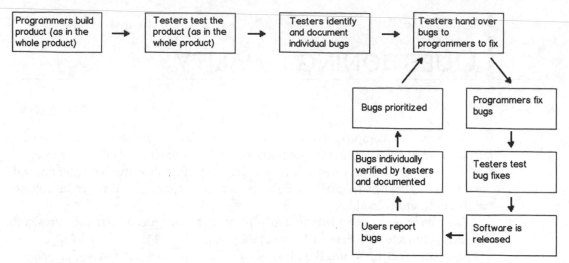

FIGURE 6.1   A simplified flow of how bugs were sequentially handled in the waterfall world.

Shortcut 11). Issues will therefore typically be picked up during the sprint (that the corresponding user story is being worked on) either by the programmer, the automated build (see Shortcut 18), a tester conducting exploratory testing, or the product owner during a walkthrough (see Shortcut 12).

▪ An issue is *not* a product backlog item (PBI). Instead, an issue should be seen as part of the evolving acceptance criteria for a user story. Essentially, what I am saying is that until the issue is resolved, the user story is not complete, and that being the case, an issue is a part of the actual user story rather than an independent, albeit associated, product backlog item.

Definition 2: Bugs

▪ A *bug* is a bug only if it is identified *after* a user story has been completed and accepted by the product owner. Bugs will therefore typically be picked up by users (postrelease) or via an automated regression test (following the implementation of subsequent user stories).

▪ A bug is a type of product backlog item. A user story is another type of product backlog item. Bugs and user stories should be prioritized together in the same product backlog and estimated using the same approach, such as relative estimation (see Shortcut 13). A particular bug may relate to a specific user story, but it should be treated independently as far as any tracking and prioritizing is concerned. To reiterate a point made in Shortcut 10, a bug can theoretically be represented utilizing the user story format, although I personally don't find it to be a suitable format in most cases.

New Principles

Now let's look at the three new principles.

Principle 1: Remove the Red Tape

Recall the second principle from the Agile Manifesto: "Working software over comprehensive documentation" (Beck et al. 2001). During my earlier years getting "soaked" in the waterfall world, I observed that a nontrivial amount of time was spent by both testers and programmers carefully documenting in painstaking detail the relevant bug minutiae. I remember regularly asking myself whether it was actually taking longer to document or to fix the damn bugs. Scrum relies on as much real-time communication as possible (rather than formalized, written bug reports), but if documentation is required, it should be fit for purpose and kept to the bare minimum.

Principle 2: Address Issues Immediately

There is nothing worse than your own stale code. Oh, wait a minute, yes there is—someone else's stale code! Sadly, back in the day when we all used to follow the sequence detailed at the beginning of the shortcut, it was very common to have to return to work on bugs in code that we had well and truly moved on from. The spin-up time to get back into the headspace to address old issues (be they yours or those of a colleague who's off on vacation) is significant and, frankly, a big fat waste of time. The sooner an issue is found, the cheaper it is to fix, and that is why with Scrum, testing is completely entwined with the programming.

Principle 3: It Ain't Over 'Til It's Over

Bottom line is that unless a user story meets the definition of done (see Shortcut 11), it might as well not exist as far as the customer is concerned. Customers are simply interested in final results and obtaining business value. If a user story is not yet done, it needs to be the top priority for the developer(s) working on it, and they should avoid moving on to any new work until it is completely done and dusted!

New Approaches

With our new bug-handling foundations now established thanks to the previous definitions and principles, let's focus on some approaches that I recommend you follow within the sprint:

- **Scenario 1: A tester is conducting some final exploratory testing on a user story and discovers an issue.**

    First, because the user story should be the top priority of the programmer working on it (see Principle 3), the tester should feel free to walk over to the programmer and explain and/or demonstrate the issue as soon as it is found. Again, because the user story is the top priority, the programmer should drop whatever he or she is doing and immediately jump on the issue. In this situation, there isn't any requirement for written documentation, as the verbal discussion will suffice, assuming that the issue is immediately resolved and verified.

■ **Scenario 2: Same as Scenario 1, but this time, the programmer in question is already in the middle of resolving a different issue (related to the same user story).**

In this case, the tester, after finding another issue, looks over and sees the programmer with headphones firmly in place and in the zone fixing a previous issue. The last thing the tester wants to do is to disturb the programmer mid-fix. As such, it is important to capture the details somewhere so that the tester can continue with the exploratory testing without forgetting the details of the new issue.

As discussed in the definition of *issue*, an issue should be treated as part of the acceptance criteria of the user story, saving the tester the pain of creating a new bug, classifying it, assigning it, prioritizing it, and so on. Instead, my recommendation is that the tester simply add a line item to the acceptance criteria with a date/time reference, initial it, and add some bullet point details of the issue. When the programmer is free, a discussion can take place using the notes as a prompt. Also, the documentation ensures that the programmer can get on with the resolution even if the tester is not around for whatever reason.

■ **Scenario 3: During the final user acceptance testing for a release, a range of trivial user interface bugs are found that were somehow missed during development.**

Again, let's try to reduce the time spent on unnecessary administration; in this situation, I recommend that a single PBI be created as a container for the collection of minor bugs. Each specific fix may take only minutes, so creating individual PBIs for each issue could end up taking longer than the actual fix-ups!

I recommend following this approach only if

- The trivial bugs are of a similar priority level.

- They are somewhat related and it makes sense to tackle them at the same time.

If these conditions aren't met, then simply create separate PBIs for the items even if they are seemingly trivial in their own right.

■ **Scenario 4: During a sprint, a critical bug is found in production requiring some of the Scrum team to resolve it.**

The first question to ask is, *How critical is critical, or more specifically, can it wait until the next sprint?* As detailed in Shortcut 1, the last thing you want to do is to change the goal of the sprint. Assuming that the production bug can wait, it should be captured as a PBI, entered into the product backlog, prioritized by the product owner, and tackled potentially in the next sprint planning session.

However, what should happen if the discovered product bug is one of those dreaded villains that simply can't wait? Well, we then need to ask another question: *How long will it take to fix the bug?* If you recall from Shortcut 8, it isn't wise to max out team capacity for working exclusively on new sprint tasks to provide some room for handling non-project-related disruptions. As such, this buffer time can also be allocated to resolve the occasional emergency bug without disrupting the sprint.

If, however, the resolution will take longer than the buffer time, you have two choices. First, you can treat these issues as impediments and track them accordingly (see Shortcut 9), or, if the issue is such a major drama (to the extent that it completely destroys the sprint goal), there is always the undesirable fallback position: a sprint cancellation that can be called by the product owner. A cancellation will end the current sprint and send the team back to sprint planning.

Turning Moths into Butterflies

Bugs can certainly cause pain, and like it or not, they're never going to become an extinct species. However, what we have learned are better ways to deal with them. We now know that disposing of fresh bugs is easier than having to deal with old, festering ones and that spending unnecessary time documenting every issue is a waste of time.

Scrum handles testing and bugs very differently from traditional approaches. By adopting these new definitions and principles, you will start to avoid the unnecessary overhead and communication breakdowns that have previously stopped teams from turning those moths into less ugly butterflies.

Shortcut 17: We Still Love the Testers!

In fact, not only do we still love the testers, we love them even more in our new Scrum world! I really feel that this is an important point to emphasize, and I'll tell you why.

I remember when I was excitedly presenting Scrum 101 concepts to my first soon-to-be Scrum team. I was sure everyone was going to pick up on my infectious enthusiasm, and indeed I gleaned a whole bunch of decisive nods and smiles. However, when I looked more closely, I started to also observe some noticeable fidgeting and darting eyes (synonymous with discomfort and fear) among a few of the testers. To understand this discomfort, we need to look into the past and briefly explore what has happened to the testing function in recent times.

Waterfall Friendship

Thanks in large part to the earlier adoption of the traditional waterfall model, a more profound appreciation for the testing function began to take hold. Within many organizations, a strong, independent testing team that stood on more of an equal footing with the programming team was becoming the norm. Testing standards were developed, professional development paths purely for testers were established, and the test team "owned" a whole phase of the cascading waterfall process.

Then along comes Scrum (and its other agile cousins), and all of a sudden, life changes. Testing becomes the responsibility of everyone on the team, unit testing becomes a programmer-centric practice, and even functional tests can be automated by programmers. Suddenly the question starts creeping into worried minds: *How and where do the testers fit in?* Before going on, and to avoid any undue panic for readers at this stage, I will cut straight to the chase and state that the tester has never been so important. Lisa Crispin and Janet Gregory (2009), authors of *Agile Testing*, emphasize that the whole-team approach is one of the biggest differences between agile development and traditional development. Some testers recognize this difference and are immediately relieved and excited by Scrum, and others remain fearful of the new world order.

Change Is in the Air

Change is scary. Crispin and Gregory offer some important insight into why the transition to agile development can be particularly worrisome for some testers. They contend that "loss of identity fear" is at the heart of a tester's concerns, and following is a selection of these specific fears:

- Fear that they will lose their QA identity

- Fear that they lack the skills to work in an agile team and will lose their jobs

- Fear that when they're dispersed into development teams, they won't get the support they need (Crispin and Gregory 2009)

As I will explain, when working in a genuine Scrum environment, none of these fears are justified. Yes, there is an identity shift; however, all of the worthy testers I have worked with have either immediately or eventually embraced their enhanced identity with open arms.

When change occurs, it is a natural instinct to romanticize the past, clinging to anything that was warm and fuzzy rather than remembering the darker, negative times. Testers shouldn't forget that life certainly wasn't a walk in the park in the old days (even if there were pretty waterfalls along the way). An image that I have etched into my memory is that of the frazzled, worn-out testers at the end of a waterfall project. "Traditional test teams are accustomed to fast and furious testing at the end of a project . . . in agile projects, you are encouraged to work at a sustainable pace" (Crispin and Gregory 2009).

New Identities

How do we help testers embrace their role in the new world where the waterfalls have dried up?

Let's first address the elephant in the room: the fear of being made functionally redundant. Fundamentally, the testers should feel safe because they are different. They possess a unique skill set and a way of thinking that is critical to the success of any software project. I like to use the description offered by Nick Jenkins in "A Software Testing Primer" (2008) to help illustrate this point:

> There is a particular philosophy that accompanies "good testing." A professional tester approaches a product with the attitude that the product is already broken—it has defects and it is their job to discover them. . . . Developers approach software with an optimism based on the assumption that the changes they make are the correct solution to a particular problem. . . . By taking a skeptical approach, the tester offers a balance. They seek to illuminate the darker part of the projects with the light of inquiry.

In a nutshell, testers think in alternative problem-solving patterns that are, generally speaking, mutually exclusive to the way programmers think.

Now that we've got that big concern out of the way, let's explore some of the exciting new subidentities that a Scrum tester can assume that are clearly above and beyond the mind numbing, repetitive manual testing that previously played such a disproportionately large part in a tester's life (see Figure 6.2).

The Tester as a Consultant

Testers are specialists at their craft, and as such, they are in a unique position to help guide nontesters to improve their testing game. With Scrum's focus on delivering quality working software on a regular basis, this has never been so important. For starters, the tester can (and should) act as a sounding board for the programmers as they start to get their heads around test-driven development.

Also, while pair programming is certainly a powerful Extreme Programming (XP) technique (that is sometimes adopted by Scrum teams), I feel that "pair testing"

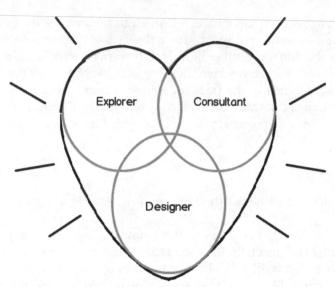

FIGURE 6.2   In Scrum, we still love the testers, especially with their new Scrum identities.

(when a tester pairs up with a programmer) is potentially even more powerful because there is additional scope to encourage functional skills transfer. It also fosters further appreciation for one another's skills and abilities.

Consulting to the user-experience designers can also be of significant benefit by helping to anticipate potential issues associated with the more complex workflows.

Finally, the product owner can no doubt leverage the tester's inherent understanding of the core acceptance criteria by assisting in various intra-sprint walkthroughs (see Shortcut 12) and helping with the final verification of the done user stories.

The Tester as a Designer

I believe that the core skill of a tester is actually that of design. Irrespective of who actually runs or implements a test, a seasoned professional tester will always be able to design the most effective test cases compared to anyone else on the team.

Well-designed tests not only form the foundation for the eventual testing itself but can also provide vital input into the technical design that takes place during sprint planning. When a tester is involved in the design of a user story's test cases prior to the sprint planning session, I can assure you that the meeting will be a great deal smoother and faster with fewer contentious debates. For those concerned that this advice is slipping into the realm of waterfalling sprints, I support Mike Cohn's (2009) thoughts:

Being part of the team on this (current) sprint and spending some time looking ahead is not the same as working a sprint ahead of the team. . . . their top priority is delivering whatever is committed for the current sprint. Beyond that, their job is to look ahead in exactly the same way everyone expects a product owner to be looking ahead.

The Tester as an Explorer

As you will read in Shortcut 18, test automation is integral to the success of Scrum. However, even with extremely thorough test automation in place, there will always be the need for manual exploratory testing that no level of automation is able to replicate. This element of testing is without doubt more art than science, and for those under the false impression that exploratory testing is just another name for gorilla or ad hoc testing, the following commentary by Crispin and Gregory (2009) will give you a new appreciation for the subtlety of this function:

> With exploratory testing, each tester has a different approach to a problem, and has a unique style of working. However, there are certain attributes that make for a good exploratory tester. A good tester:
>
> - Is systematic, but pursues "smells" (anomalies, pieces that aren't consistent).
> - Learns to recognize problems through the use of Oracles (principle or mechanism by which we recognize a problem).
> - Chooses a theme or role or mission statement to focus testing.
> - Time-boxes sessions and side trips.
> - Thinks about what the expert or novice user would do.
> - Explores together with domain experts.
> - Checks out similar or competitive applications.

A New Beginning

In a Scrum team, everyone is responsible for testing. Quality is no longer an afterthought, and testing should become an inherent part of every stage of the user story development, including before a single line of functional code is written.

The transition to Scrum should feel like an exciting rebirth for the tester. Removing the manual testing shackles offers Scrum testers an opportunity to focus on what they do best: design, consulting, and exploratory testing. They are finally given an opportunity to flex their unique skill set in far more interesting ways than before.

Shortcut 18: Automation Nation

You've got a simple choice: jump on the automation bandwagon, destined for exciting Scrum-filled destinations or suffer a trip down the slippery slopes of "Scrummer-fall."

Trying to implement Scrum without automation is like trying to drive a sports car on a beaten-up dirt track—you won't experience the full potential of your exciting vehicle, you will get horribly frustrated, and no doubt you will end up damaging and probably blaming the car. As James Shore and Shane Warden (2007) point out,

> Software development is demanding. It requires perfection, consistently, for months and years of effort. At best, mistakes lead to code that won't compile. At worst, they lead to bugs that lie in wait and pounce at the moment that does the most damage.

The Scrum Guide, written by Ken Schwaber and Jeff Sutherland, doesn't make mention of software engineering practices at all; in fact, the words *software* and *engineering* do not appear once in the guide. Rather, Scrum is abstracted above this layer, described more generically as a "framework for developing and sustaining complex products" (Schwaber and Sutherland 2011).

That being said, you won't hear one genuine expert say that Scrum (as it applies in the software context) doesn't work significantly better when it is combined with strong, automated software engineering practices such as those that you will find in the Extreme Programming (XP) set of practices (Beck 1999). This shortcut explains why.

Automation is a massive topic—numerous books are dedicated to it exclusively. This shortcut simply gives you some general advice to start you on your automation journey. There are many layers, many tools, and various combinations of tools; however, I intend to keep this shortcut nice and straightforward to avoid your getting analysis paralysis.

We focus on several key automation practices that are all heavily intertwined, including continuous integration, test automation, build/deploy automation, and the relatively new concept of continuous delivery.

Continuous Integration (CI)

Martin Fowler (2006), one of the original signatories to the Agile Manifesto, describes the core practice of continuous integration:

> Continuous Integration is a software development practice where members of a team integrate their work frequently, usually each person integrates at least daily—leading to multiple integrations per day. Each integration is verified by an automated build (including test) to detect integration errors as quickly as possible.

What's the key benefit, then (if it's not already obvious)? Again, I don't think I can describe it any better than Fowler does:

> Integration is a long and unpredictable process . . . . The trouble with deferred integration is that it's very hard to predict how long it will take to do, and worse, it's very hard to see how far you are through the process. The result is that you

are putting yourself into a complete blind spot right at one of the [most tense] parts of a project—even if you're one of the rare cases where you aren't already late.

Getting CI up and running is certainly a great place to start your automation journey. Scrum trainer, Kane Mar (2012) further emphasizes this point: "Developing an increment of potentially shippable code without CI is almost impossible after the 3rd or 4th sprint simply because the amount of change and regression testing becomes overwhelming." CI is a classic embodiment of the proverb, "A stitch in time saves nine." By frequently ironing out any small integration issues on a day-to-day basis rather than battling a vast array of compounding integration problems at the end of a project, teams save themselves from considerable stress and anguish.

The CI server constantly monitors for any new code that, when checked in, automatically triggers a new build. In the process, the server can (and should) be configured to run any automated tests. Because numerous CI builds will be run every day, it is critical to ensure that the build is very quick—any longer than 10 to 15 minutes will cause bottlenecks in development and defeat the whole purpose. This 10- to 15-minute time constraint could mean that the CI build won't include all of the slower functional tests that instead get run during the secondary build (we cover this topic later in the shortcut).

Test Automation

It doesn't take a genius to work out what will happen if test automation isn't introduced. By about sprint 3 or 4, the amount of manual regression testing will become so significant that some team members may feel tempted to resort to running a dedicated " testing sprint" (see Figure 6.3). This is not a good idea, but even worse, some

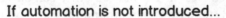

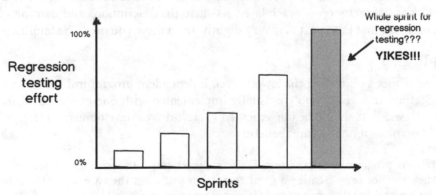

FIGURE 6.3   If test automation is not introduced, a "testing sprint" could be just around the corner.

bright spark may even suggest that a "testing team" should work a sprint (or more) behind to catch up on the regression testing. If either of these situations occur, your team has begun the sad decline back into the nonincremental world of traditional waterfall development.

The good news is that with test automation, there is no reason to fear slipping back to the dark ages. The bad news, as Crispin and Gregory (2009) explain, is that "automation requires a big investment, one that may not pay off right away. It takes time and research to decide on what test frameworks to use and whether to build them in-house or use externally produced tools."

While I agree that an investment is needed, I am also a firm believer that the positives far outweigh the negatives. Some of the benefits provided by Crispin and Gregory include the following:

- Manual testing takes too long.

- Manual processes are error prone.

- Automation frees people to do their best work.

- Automated regression tests provide a safety net.

- Automated tests give feedback early and often.

- Tests and examples that drive coding can do more.

- Tests provide documentation.

- Automation can be a good return on investment.

Types of Automated Testing

It can be a little daunting when you are first introduced to the vast world of test automation. Not only are there numerous test layers, but the other complication is that there is still a lack of industry-level standardization around the naming conventions as well as the exact scope of each layer. As such, the descriptions and naming of the various layers that I use next may vary slightly from those you might be familiar with.

Unit Testing

Unit tests focus on testing the lowest-level, independent programming blocks (such as a method in a class) and are usually implemented with one of the xUnit frameworks. These tests should be implemented via test-driven development (TDD), which provides an additional spinoff benefit:

> If your programmers are using TDD as a mechanism to write their tests, then they are not only creating a great regression suite, but they are using them to design high-quality, robust code (Crispin and Gregory 2009).

For those of you who are unfamiliar with TDD, Ron Jeffries (2010), Agile Manifesto signatory and Scrum trainer, offers a great explanation:

> Test-Driven Development requires me to write all the code, and only the code, that is needed to pass tests, which I write first. This discipline helps me focus on what the code must do before I focus on how it would do it, and it results in code which is simple and quite testable. TDD is not a rote, stupid practice. It is, instead, an almost meditative way of keeping my mind focused on what's going on. It reduces my defects a lot, and my tension even more.

Functional Testing

Functional testing is also often called *acceptance testing*. Perhaps one day we will call it *user story testing*, as the idea is to be able to test and automate the full end-to-end functionality of a particular user story.

These types of tests may or may not include automating the testing of the user interface (UI). This additional layer typically incurs additional cost because of the time it takes to run tests through the UI, not to mention its potential fragility (the UI is frequently adjusted throughout development). For those who wish to test just behind the UI, tools such as FitNesse[1] are very effective, whereas to test through all of the layers, tools like Selenium[2] can be utilized. Both FitNesse and Selenium are open source and freely available.

Integration Testing

Often also called *system testing*, integration testing is all about ensuring that new functionality is able to play nicely with the broader ecosystem and not just in isolation. For example, the product under development may need to integrate with other internal products such as administrative tools or with third-party products such as payment gateways.

Performance Testing

Other aliases also exist for performance testing: *load testing* and *stress testing*. The focus of performance testing is to measure the operation of the product when under pressure, typically brought about by increasing the number of users and/or increasing the amount of data processing required.

Note that unless you are actually releasing to production every sprint (or more frequently), you may not need to run performance testing every sprint. "Special-purpose types of testing such as integration testing, performance testing, usability testing, and so on may not be performed every sprint" (Cohn 2009). That being said, don't make the intervals between integration and performance test runs too long because issues found late may require a trip back to the drawing board.

---

1. For more information about FitNesse, go to http://en.wikipedia.org/wiki/Fitnesse.
2. For more information about Selenium, go to http://en.wikipedia.org/wiki/Selenium_(software).

Deployment Automation

If you think that getting Scrum up and running in a nice, pristine development environment is good enough, then it's time for a reality check. If your team is unable to push their work with extreme confidence, at the touch of a button, out of the nice, safe development cradle into the big, bad production environment, then you should consider your delineated phased approach to be another form of Scrummer-fall. Simply put, your team must do its utmost to completely automate the build-deploy process for all environments being used.

With that in mind, let's look at the typical key environments and how they relate to the different automated tests.

Development Environment

Earlier in the shortcut, we focused on the benefits of the CI server and the fact that it should be able to automatically run a build after every check-in.

In addition to running the CI build, I recommend running a secondary build in the development environment (traditionally known as the *nightly build*) that is triggered manually and less frequently. The difference between the CI build and the secondary build is that the latter should be given the luxury of time, and therefore, it can include the full set of tests (including all of the heavier functional and UI tests that take significantly longer to run). Shore and Warden (2007) point out some further functions that the secondary build should perform:

> In addition to compiling your source code and running tests, it should configure registry settings, initialize database schemas, set up web servers, launch processes—everything you need to build and test your software from scratch without human intervention.

The big trick here is to ensure that the development environment resembles the staging and production environments as closely as possible. For various reasons, such as licensing and speed, you may not be able to replicate all associated components, but you should still be able to stub them out using mock objects to at least simulate reality. Also, even if it is unlikely that you would replicate the entire production dataset (say, to save time, if it is of considerable size), the dataset used in the development environment should be at least representative of the real one as far as data integrity is concerned.

Why is this effort so important? By performing repeated dress rehearsals of your release into production, your system testing is happening every day rather than at the end of the release when remedial time is considerably limited.

Staging Environment

Although the development environment should at least mimic the production environment, your staging environment should be *identical* to it. The full dataset as well as all applicable third-party products and components that the product interacts with should be represented here.

In this environment, further integration testing can take place, and it is also often the primary location where performance tests are run.

Continuous Delivery and Scrum

A growing number of people in the agile community are adopting approaches such as *continuous deployment* or *continuous delivery*. Although the terms are often used interchangeably, Jez Humble (2010), coauthor of *Continuous Delivery*, explains the difference between the two:

> While continuous deployment implies continuous delivery the converse is not true. Continuous delivery is about putting the release schedule in the hands of the business, not in the hands of IT. Implementing continuous delivery means making sure your software is always production ready throughout its entire life-cycle—that any build could *potentially* be released to users at the touch of a button using a fully automated process in a matter of seconds or minutes (Humble 2010).

So, while continuous delivery makes every build *releasable* to users, continuous deployment actually *releases* every change to users (sometimes multiple times a day).

I mention these approaches because I wish to dispel a couple of myths. The first myth is that Scrum and continuous deployment/delivery are mutually exclusive. In some quarters there appears to be the perception that if you use Scrum, you can release only at the end of the sprint. This is not the case. Scrum talks about having releasable product increments at the end of the sprint, but that doesn't mean you can't also release *during* the sprint—simply make it part of the definition of done (if it applies across the board) or part of the acceptance criteria for a specific user story if it has release urgency.

The other myth I hear frequently is that some people believe Scrum dictates that you *must* release to production at the end of every sprint. Again, this is not true, and those who believe it need to appreciate the difference between the words *release* and *releasable*. Scrum does not say that you must release at the end of every sprint, but it does say that you should do everything possible to have something releasable at the end of a sprint.

Every Journey Begins with But a Small Step

Just start somewhere. I know that even after reading a brief shortcut like this one, you might feel that it all sounds too hard. If that is how you're feeling, please realize that in the case of automation, something really is better than nothing. One unit test is better than no unit tests. An automated build that takes 30 minutes is better than one that takes hours of manual work.

I recommend that if you are new to automation, you allocate a percentage of your sprint capacity to chipping away at it. Start with CI. Then automate the rest of your builds. Next, focus on applying unit tests to all new critical code, and then expand to all new code. Your next step could then be retrofitting old code with some more all-encompassing functional tests.

The choice is yours; however, either way, start somewhere and remember that without automation, you lose time, and worse than that, you are relying on fallible and time-constrained humans. To reinforce Shore and Warden's earlier quote regarding perfection, I close this shortcut with a classic from Frederick Brooks, author of *The Mythical Man-Month* (1995):

> Human beings are not accustomed to being perfect, and few areas of human activity demand it. Adjusting to the requirement for perfection is, I think, the most difficult part of learning to program.

Wrap Up

The three shortcuts included in this chapter focused on a selection of tactics, tools, and tips to help your team track and manage defects on a Scrum project. Let's recap what was covered:

Shortcut 16: Bah! Scrum Bug!

- Differentiating between bugs and issues

- A selection of underlying defect-handling principles to consider

- Approaches for tracking and managing defects within sprints

Shortcut 17: We Still Love the Testers!

- The evolution of the tester role

- Why specialized testers are still vital for high-performing Scrum teams

- Key functions that a tester should focus on: consulting, designing. and exploring

Shortcut 18: Automation Nation

- The importance of automation to avoid slipping back into waterfall patterns

- A selection of automation starting points

- How Scrum and continuous delivery play nicely together

Chapter 7
MONITORING AND METRICS

Ensuring that a Scrum project stays on track requires frequent tuning and fine-tuning. Thankfully, Scrum's core set of sprint activities provides us with regular opportunities to monitor progress. Anecdotal observation can be greatly assisted with a selection of carefully selected metrics, tracking boards, and team synchronization practices.

The following three shortcuts focus on some useful techniques and tools to help gauge how your project is shaping up.

Shortcut 19: Metrics That Matter provides a selection of effective metrics that can be used for gauging ongoing progress. Shortcut 20: Outstanding Stand-Ups offers a selection of tips and tricks to ensure that the daily scrum doesn't become an endless talk-fest. Finally, Shortcut 21: Taming the Task Board provides advice for getting the most out of your team's visual centerpiece.

Shortcut 19: Metrics That Matter

You've introduced Scrum and your team is out of the blocks, sprinting away! Things are going pretty well until some wise guy from senior management comes up to you and says something along the lines of, "Sooo, this whole Scrum thing sounds great in theory, but what metrics are you going to use to actually demonstrate to us how effective it really is?"

Like it or not, people just love to measure and compare, so when it comes to avoiding metrics, you can run, but you can't hide. In this shortcut, I offer you some suggestions about what metrics actually matter when it comes to implementing Scrum.

Types of Metrics

The most important piece of advice that I can offer when it comes to metrics is to use them only for good, *not* for evil. Considering that there aren't any readily available global definitions of *good metric* and *evil metric*, I have come up with my own:

- **Good metric:** Used as a signal to help the team identify roughly where things are at and, more importantly, as a guide to help the team inspect and adapt its processes to improve over time

- **Evil metric:** Used as an inflexible indicator for micromanaging an individual's performance over time and, more importantly, for beating people up and killing morale

I look at grouping metrics into two main categories:

- **Metrics for Scrum projects** (the focus of this shortcut)
- **Metrics for broader Scrum rollouts** (the focus of Shortcut 28)

Four Meaningful Metrics

The following sections walk you through a selection of four project-related metrics that I find particularly helpful:

- Sprint burndown
- Enhanced release burndown
- Sprint interference
- Remedial focus

Sprint Burndown

The sprint burndown is a forecasting metric that assists in tracking progress throughout the current sprint.

How Is It Generated?

The sprint burndown is generated in the following manner:

1. For each day in a sprint, plot the sum of the remaining times for all tasks in the sprint backlog.

2. Draw a connecting line between the current day's total and the previous day's total (see Figure 7.1).

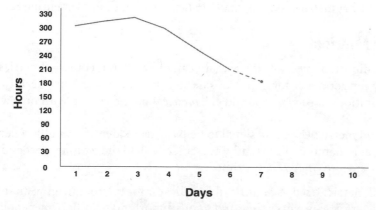

FIGURE 7.1 A sprint burndown chart, updated on a daily basis.

When Is It Generated?

The sprint burndown is generated at the end of each day of a sprint, excluding the final day, which is dedicated to the sprint review, the sprint retrospective, and planning for the subsequent sprint *(see Shortcut 8)*.

What Is It Telling You?

The sprint burndown metric acts as a daily gauge for the Scrum team to help manage its workflow and track progress.

If the chart is trending behind schedule (see Figure 7.2), it could be reflecting the fact that

- New tasks were added to the sprint backlog (that weren't anticipated during sprint planning).
- Some of the task estimations were incorrect.
- Team members had taken some unplanned time off.
- Impediments had hampered progress.

Of course, it is possible that all four factors had come into play, causing the now expected delay.

Following sprint planning, many teams draw a straight, diagonal (theoretical) line from the top of the *y*-axis values to end of the *x*-axis values and use it as a benchmark for the actual burndown line. I warn against using this approach because it can easily create an inaccurate perception of progress. The problem with this line is that sprint progress rarely mirrors the theoretical line on a day-to-day basis. Many sprint

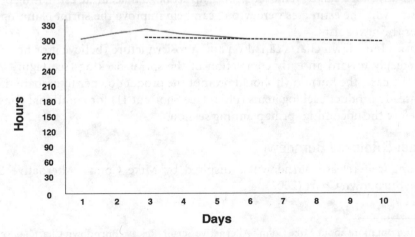

FIGURE 7.2   The team is clearly behind schedule; time to speak to the product owner about possibly decreasing scope.

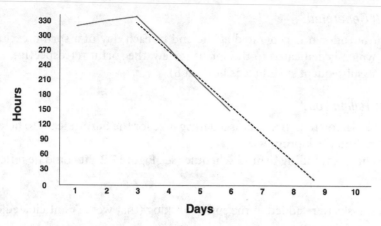

FIGURE 7.3   The team is clearly ahead of schedule; time to speak to the product owner about adding scope.

burndown lines actually burn up for the first few days because of new discoveries before beginning their downward descent as the team gathers momentum. By including the theoretical line, a curious stakeholder may get the misleading impression that the team has fallen behind after only a day or two.

How Can You Act On It?

If the sprint burndown clearly indicates that the team is not going to reach the sprint goal, then apart from doing everything in your power to help remove any impediments (see Shortcut 9), you should have a discussion with the product owner to assess whether any scope can be removed. If the slip is due to inaccurate estimating of tasks, analyzing why the estimates were wrong can help improve the sprint planning accuracy for the next sprint.

Sprint burndown charts can also paint a rosier picture (believe it or not) if they trend steeply toward an early completion of the sprint backlog (see Figure 7.3). If this is the case, the burndown should prompt the product owner to prepare the next sprint-ready product backlog items (PBIs) (see Shortcut 11) for additional consumption before the upcoming sprint planning session.

Enhanced Release Burndown

The enhanced release burndown is inspired by Mike Cohn's Alternative Scrum Release Burndown Chart (2002).[1]

---

1. To find out more about Mike Cohn's Alternative Scrum Release Burndown Chart, go to www.mountaingoatsoftware.com/scrum/alt-releaseburndown/.

How Is It Generated?

The enhanced release burndown chart is generated in the following manner:

1. For each sprint, plot the sum of the remaining points for all PBIs in the product backlog designated for the next release.

2. Draw a trend line relating to the data points in step 1.

3. For each sprint, plot (as negative y-axis values) the sum of the story points for any PBIs added to the product backlog after the start of the project (if applicable).

4. Draw another trend line that relates to the data points in step 3 (see Figure 7.4).

When Is It Generated?

The enhanced release burndown metric is generated at the end of every sprint.

What Is It Telling You?

This metric signals what the development team's rate of progress is relative to the scope's rate of change. The point where the two trend lines (hopefully) intersect indicates roughly how many sprints will be required to complete the release. If the trend lines run parallel to each other (or diverge), it is an ominous indication that the release will theoretically never see the light of day (see Figure 7.5).

How Can You Act On It?

If the two trend lines do not intersect or the expected release duration is intolerable, then either the rate of progress needs to increase (by improving practices and/or removing impediments) or the scope needs to be reduced.

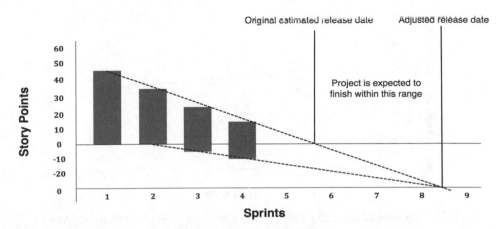

FIGURE 7.4   An enhanced burndown chart, updated after each sprint.

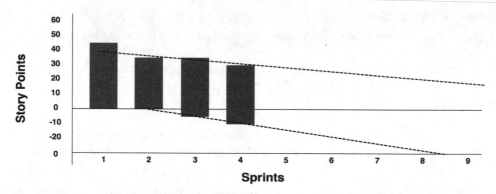

FIGURE 7.5   Ominous signs that this release might never see the light of day. Better improve practices, remove impediments, or decrease scope.

Sprint Interference

Sprint interference is a productivity metric that assists teams with their sprint capacity planning.

How Is It Generated?

Sprint interference is generated in the following manner:

1. For each sprint, plot the sum of the time spent by any of the developers for any non-sprint backlog tasks.

2. Draw a trend line that relates to the data points in step 1 (see Figure 7.6).

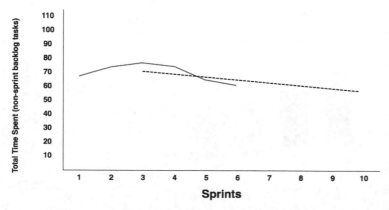

FIGURE 7.6   Be sure to note the trend in this graph to assist in estimating your team's capacity at the next sprint planning session.

When Is It Generated?

The sprint interference metric is generated during sprint planning.

What Is It Telling You?

By providing visibility on the time spent handling historical sprint disruptions, this metric helps you to estimate the potential sprint capacity for the upcoming sprint (the amount of time that the development team should allocate to sprint backlog tasks). This is especially helpful if you have adopted commitment-based sprint planning (see Shortcut 8).

How Can You Act On It?

In any given sprint, there will be a range of external organizational disruptions that simply can't be avoided. This metric assists in quantifying these disruptions and can also indirectly help to identify what are unavoidable disruptions (such as company meetings) and what are avoidable impediments (such as constantly having to fix inadequate equipment).

Remedial Focus

Remedial focus is a quality metric that enables teams to gauge how much of their collective effort is being spent on remedial bug-fixing as opposed to working on new requirements.

How Is It Generated?

Remedial focus is generated in the following manner:

1. For each sprint, plot the total velocity (the sum of the points for all PBIs including both new functionality and bugs).

2. For each sprint, plot the sum of the points for all bug-related work.

3. Draw a trend line that relates to the data points in step 2 (see Figure 7.7).

When Is It Generated?

The remedial focus metric is generated at the end of each sprint.

What Is It Telling You?

This metric monitors the fluctuations in product quality by measuring the percentage of each sprint that is spent working on bugs as opposed to new functional requirements.

In addition, by quantifying the makeup of the total velocity, additional insight can be garnered. For example, the total velocity may be trending upward, which on the surface would indicate positive improvement. However, if the amount of bug-related work is also trending upward, it indicates that the level of quality is slipping (see Figure 7.8).

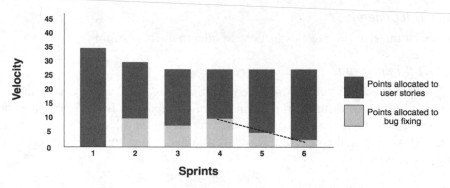

FIGURE 7.7   This indicates that quality is improving. The effort spent on bug-fixing is going down while velocity remains consistent.

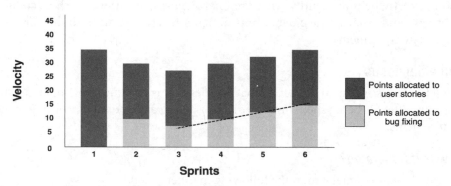

FIGURE 7.8   Even though velocity is increasing, it's not all good news, as quality is decreasing. Time to revisit the definition of done.

As such, the increase in total velocity could in fact indicate that the team is just getting faster at fixing its own bugs—somewhat of a backhanded compliment.

How Can We Act On It?

If the time spent on bugs isn't trending downward, it is a clear indication that the level of inherent quality is insufficient. This should prompt the Scrum team to revisit the definition of done to tighten up the quality requirements.

Beware of Analysis Paralysis

These four metrics form a small subset of the potential metrics that can be derived and utilized during a Scrum project. But be warned: incessantly generating metrics (just because you can) may cause you to contract an illness that Scrum on the whole tries to combat—analysis paralysis.

Finally, it is vitally important to reinforce the point that metrics need to be handled with care and used for good, not for evil. Use metrics as signals to help your team improve their practices and definitely not for micromanaging and measuring individual performance.

Shortcut 20: Outstanding Stand-Ups

Ask anyone in the sales department what Scrum is, and apart from mentioning the colorful, sticky-note-decorated task board (see Shortcut 21), they will more than likely mention the daily scrum, also known as the team stand-up.

The daily scrum is the regular pulse of the team. A pulse needs to be steady, consistent, and lively to remain healthy, and this shortcut gives you a few tips to help ensure that these sessions keep humming along like clockwork.

When and Where?

First things first: I highly recommend that the daily scrum be conducted as a stand-up rather than a sit-down. It is a subtle yet important distinction. The simple act of standing provides the team with a sense of liveliness to help kick-start the day, and it also ensures that the session stays short and sharp to prevent aching legs!

I am not a believer in imposing the time of the daily scrum on the team: the time should be decided as a group. However, you should encourage everyone to commit to a time that works for them that is as early as possible in the day. Of course, if your team is disparately located, then your daily scrum time will need to accommodate the various time zones.

Once there is an agreed-upon time, you can start to reinforce some guidelines. Here are three that I am a fan of:

- The daily scrum should start on the dot irrespective of who is late.

- Anyone who is late without either prior warning, a super excuse, or an extremely funny excuse (that induces laughter from every team member) needs to make a financial contribution to the late jar (this can go toward an agreed-upon charity).

- Your daily scrum should look like a nice tight circle (or semicircle around the task board) rather than an amorphous blob (see Figure 7.9).

FIGURE 7.9 Your daily scrum should look like a nice tight circle (or semicircle) instead of an amorphous blob.

What Should Be Covered?

The typical questions that each developer answers during the daily scrum are

- What did I achieve yesterday?
- What do I hope to achieve today?
- Do I have any impediments or blocks?

Although these questions seem straightforward, I have a few specific tips to make your daily scrums more effective. First, everyone should reference the tasks on the task board when discussing what they achieved and what they hope to achieve. This way, you ensure that the task board is up to date (if anyone forgot the night before).

In reality, it should take each team member only about 30 seconds to run through the three questions. However, the problem is that at least a couple of updates every day will typically spawn spinoff discussions that can drag the entire team into a black hole of debate (until everyone realizes that their legs are aching after standing for half an hour!). It is very easy for a daily scrum to get hijacked by implementation detail, so I highly recommend that whenever you get a whiff of tangential discussion, jump in and say "offline," or if you want to be more subtle, slowly start raising your hand. What you are communicating with this prompt is the following: "I know that this is an important discussion, but let's get through all of the updates, and then at the end, anyone who is *required* to participate in the discussion can hang back."

GIFTS

Agile consultant and blogger Jason Yip explains the key purpose of the stand-up using an apt acronym, GIFTS (Yip 2011), which I like as a simple mnemonic:

Good Start—**Good Start** means that the stand-up meeting should give energy, not take it. Energy comes from instilling a sense of purpose and urgency.

Improvement—We can't fix problems we don't know about so a large part of stand-ups is about exposing problems to allow us to improve. **Improvement** is not just about problem solving though. Sharing better techniques and ideas is also important.

Focus—The stand-up should encourage a **focus** on moving work through the system in order to achieve our objectives, not encourage pointless activity.

Team—Effective **teams** are built by regularly communicating, working, and helping each other. This is also strongly tied with team members helping each other with shared obstacles.

Status—**Status** is about answering a couple questions:

How is the work progressing?

Is there anything else interesting that the team should know?

Multiple Teams

Your project may include multiple parallel Scrum teams that share common inter-faces (both technical and communicative). A popular option in this situation is to run a scrum of scrums stand-up (an additional stand-up with a representative from each team). This is a good option, but I personally prefer the use of *stand-up ambassadors* who act as observers in the other groups to pick up on any potential contention and/or lessons (see Figure 7.10). This way, there are fewer potential breakpoints in the communication channel. These ambassadors are typically the most senior developers in each of the groups. If you adopt this approach, it is important to stagger the kick-off times of each team's daily scrum so that ambassadors can attend.

Ignore the ScrumMaster

I like the way Ken Schwaber (2004) puts it when he states that the daily scrum is sup-posed to be an opportunity for the group to briefly "socialize and synchronize." It is not a roll call or micromanagement session where the team reports into the Scrum-Master and/or product owner. I often find that some team members get into the habit of directing their update to the ScrumMaster only. If you notice a team member addressing the ScrumMaster without making eye contact with anyone else, a tip is to start slowly turning around or looking up at the ceiling—I have found that the habit is quickly broken with this physical cue.

Some Extra Touches

I recommend that before the daily scrum formalities begin, encourage (but don't contrive) any light banter and joking around—it's always nice to start the day on a positive note feeling energized instead of feeling like you're at a military roll call!

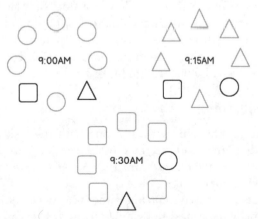

FIGURE 7.10   Stagger the kick-off times for each team's daily scrum so that ambas-sadors can attend.

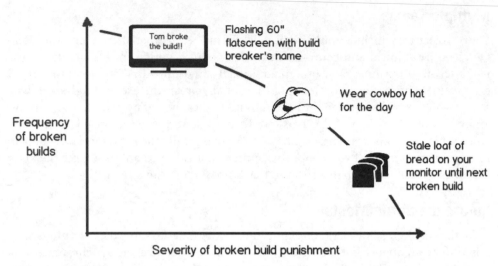

Frequency of broken builds

Severity of broken build punishment

FIGURE 7.11   Broken build "punishments" can range from innocuous to extreme.

I also like to use the daily scrum as the forum for awarding the infamous broken build punishment. The team can really flex their creative muscles when collectively determining their approach to this (see Figure 7.11). Some suggestions include anything from the relatively innocuous monitor that flashes the culprit's name to the more extreme practice of placing a moldy loaf of bread on the transgressor's monitor (Keith 2010)—this was much easier prior to flatscreens! My longstanding preference sits somewhere in the middle of this spectrum whereby the culpable party is awarded the Akubra (Australian cowboy hat) to wear for the rest of the day (including to lunch!).

While the daily scrum can certainly flow in a stock-standard direction, I like to keep everyone on their toes by utilizing some sort of randomizer. For example, you can use a small soccer ball that gets passed around from team member to team member in any order; anyone who isn't listening (or is a terrible soccer player) will get a little embarrassed as the ball slips through his or her legs.

It's Hitting the Big Time!

I see a bright future for the daily scrum. Along with the task board, it is a popular Scrum element that I'm already seeing cross the chasm into non-software-related teams to great effect; even the mainstream *Wall Street Journal* (Silverman 2012) has reported on its growing popularity!

The daily scrum is a simple concept, but without care it can quickly turn into a daily mess! So, try out some of these mess-mitigating tips, and never forget Conway's law:

Organizations which design systems . . . are constrained to produce designs which are copies of the communication structures of these organizations. (Conway 1968)

Shortcut 21: Taming the Task Board

For those sitting on the Scrum periphery, probably the most recognizable element of any Scrum project is the visual team task board. Sitting as the focal centerpiece and gathering point for the team, this colorful, sticky-note-adorned board has almost become the symbol of Scrum. With popularity comes variety, and these days there is no shortage of variations when it comes to board configuration and form factor. While there really is no right or wrong way to create your Scrum centerpiece, you won't be surprised to find that I certainly have strong opinions on the matter!

Digital or Physical?

Personally, I was a little baffled when I first saw a physical Scrum task board, utilizing low-tech, paper-based sticky-notes, marker pens, and sticky-tack! Why, oh why, would we, as bleeding-edge technical hotshots, go back to the dark ages and use antiquated tooling instead of nice, shiny, oversized monitors projecting slick charts? Well, the answer to the question is simple: human psychology. The pioneers of the task board certainly knew what they were doing when they made the simple, physical board the de facto standard.

The bottom line is that there is something satisfying and gratifying when you get up off your seat, walk to the board (it really isn't that much exercise, people), pick up a sticky-note, and slap it into the Done column. I feel that the visceral "ceremony" of this movement really appeals to our natural sense of achievement because of the visual recognition of work completed (particularly in an industry where most of the hard work is invisible to others). Also, it doesn't hurt to make the physical working environment more colorful and stimulating, does it?

Materials Needed to Go Old School

To set up a physical task board, you need the following:

- Large whiteboard/wall/pane of glass
- Blue painter's tape (to create the columns)
- Large ruler (for your rows)
- Whiteboard marker (also for your rows)
- Sticky-notes (two colors)

Setting Up Your Columns

Columns can be set up in a variety of ways. My preference is the following:

Not Started | In Progress | Ready to Verify | Done

Rows of Sticky-Notes

The rows represent the sprint backlog items, including the PBIs (and associated tasks) that will be focused on during the sprint. Don't use your tape for the rows (just the columns) because the rows will obviously vary per sprint (and retaping every couple of weeks will get very annoying). Basically, each row will be dedicated to a single PBI and its associated tasks.

Each sticky-note represents a specific task item. Try to make each constituent task of a PBI a " vertical, " independently testable slice; otherwise, the Ready to Verify column won't be as meaningful on a task-by-task basis. I talk in more detail about this task-splitting process in Shortcut 8.

Sticky-Note Content

If you are also using a software tool to help manage your Scrum artifacts, there is a fine line between wasting time replicating details (that have already been captured digitally), on the one hand, and not jotting enough detail on the sticky-notes, on the other hand. The trick is to write just enough on the note to make it identifiable. I recommend that your sticky-notes include the task ID number (that is automatically generated by the software tool), the initials of whoever has taken on the task, a few words describing the task, and the current time remaining (see Figure 7.12).

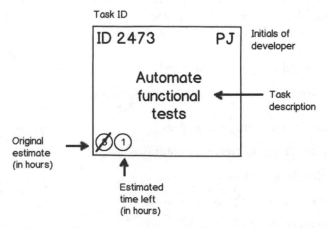

FIGURE 7.12   Example content for a sticky-note.

Any unplanned work should also be captured on the task board, though I recommend using a different-colored sticky-note (see Shortcut 12). This way you can clearly identify potential improvement areas in the sprint planning process.

Generating the Burndown

I'm a fan of the sprint burndown chart (see Shortcut 19), and if you are using Scrum software, you should be able to automatically generate it on a daily basis. However, even with this option, I prefer updating it manually. It takes less effort to extend the line by a one-day segment than to reprint another chart. In addition, I enjoy the ceremony of updating the burndown in front of the team just before officially kicking off the daily scrum, as I find it adds a healthy air of anticipation!

Some Important Decoration

There are several other artifacts that you might consider printing out in a nice big, bright font and sticking on the wall near the task board (see Figure 7.13).

Sprint Goal

The sprint goal (see Shortcut 8) is the umbrella objective that the team is aiming to achieve, so it would be remiss not to display this headline prominently.

Retrospective Goals

After the previous sprint retrospective, the team should have determined the priority process improvements to focus on in the upcoming sprint (see Shortcut 23). It's easy to

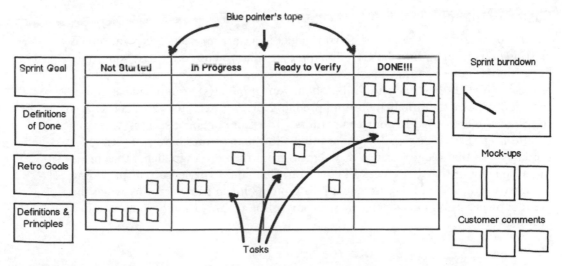

FIGURE 7.13   The task board in all its glory along with some "important decoration."

forget about these actions when the team is heavily engrossed in the actual functional work, but if these actions aren't kept front of mind, then the team will get caught in a vicious cycle where continual improvement is relegated to an afterthought. I have seen teams use a completely separate task board purely for retrospective tasks, but I recommend printing these goals out and sticking them on the project wall.

Definitions and Principles

In the early stages of a project new to Scrum, the team must absorb a lot of new information. Remember that familiar processes and definitions have been turned on their heads, and breaking habitual thinking doesn't happen overnight. To combat those old habits, displaying the new definitions of commonly referenced elements such as *impediments* (see Shortcut 9) and *bugs/issues* (see Shortcut 16) can be very helpful.

Keeping It Real!

In the very early stages of a development project, before the various user stories morph and amalgamate into a slick, well-packaged final product, the team might occasionally lose sight of the big picture and final goal. Following are a couple of suggestions to help everyone keep their eyes on the prize.

High-Level Mock-Ups

In many cases, before the first sprint has kicked off, the product owner will have worked up some high-level mock-ups of the key user interfaces (even if they are just hand-drawn sketches at this stage). Irrespective of how rough they are, it is a great idea to stick a copy of them near the task board to give everyone a constant reminder of the big picture.

Customer Quotes

Unless your team is developing the first product in a start-up, your organization has existing users who, on the whole, really appreciate what you do (otherwise you would be sitting at home playing Xbox). No doubt these users have occasionally offered feedback on what they like and dislike about your product(s). You may hear things such as, "We love the simplicity behind product ABC," or perhaps, "Product XYZ is so responsive compared to your competitors." To ensure ongoing success, it is prudent to keep these user signals front of mind. How many times have you seen great products lose their edge because they digress from the core ingredients that made them popular in the first place? I know from firsthand experience that providing visibility on these types of user quotations prompts much more scrutiny when the product owner or other stakeholders start suggesting the inclusion of that extra bell or whistle.

Party Time!

After a particularly difficult sprint, you might be pretty darn excited about throwing all of those sticky-notes straight into the nearest trash can. If trashing the notes provides you some much needed therapy, then go right ahead. However, another suggestion is to keep them all (in the bottom of some drawer) and decorate the release-party room with them for some nostalgia (or perhaps nausea)!

Although the task board might currently be perceived as an exclusive agile tool, I often discuss its efficacy with leaders operating in fields as varied as the legal profession and school teaching, so sit tight, as I don't think it will be long before these colorful boards start to take over the world!

Wrap Up

The three shortcuts discussed in this chapter focused on a selection of tactics, tools, and tips to help gauge how your project is progressing. Let's do a quick recap of what was covered:

Shortcut 19: Metrics That Matter

- Differentiating between good and evil metrics
- A selection of meaningful metrics: the sprint burndown, the enhanced release burndown, sprint interference, and remedial work effort
- The importance of avoiding metric overkill

Shortcut 20: Outstanding Stand-Ups

- Daily scrum logistics: when, where, and what should be covered
- Options for synchronizing multiple teams
- Dealing with common daily scrum dysfunctions

Shortcut 21: Taming the Task Board

- Factors to consider when deciding between a digital or physical board
- How to set up a physical task board
- Additional artifacts to consider embellishing your task board with

Chapter 8

RETROS, REVIEWS, AND RISKS

Thankfully, the days of the onerous, postmortem debrief (held at the very end of a long project when it is least helpful) are over! Instead, our Scrum projects opt for frequent inspection and adaptation of both the product and the process at the end of every sprint to ensure that risks are mitigated and lessons are being applied when they matter most.

The three shortcuts in this chapter provide suggestions for making the most of your regular sprint reviews and retrospectives.

Shortcut 22: To-Dos for Your Sprint Reviews focuses on steps to take to ensure your team doesn't sell itself short during the open sprint review. Shortcut 23: Retrospective Irrespective suggests two effective retrospective techniques as well as key areas to focus on during this end-of-sprint activity. Shortcut 24: Risk Takers and Mistake Makers discusses the need to generate a failsafe environment, which in turn generates a culture of openness and innovation.

Shortcut 22: To-Dos for Your Sprint Reviews

WARNING: On the surface, this Scrum activity appears to be both simple and straightforward. But be warned: without careful preparation, this session can lead to riotous table-thumping and streams of tears.

Just show the stakeholders what was completed over the last 2-week sprint—sounds simple right? Well, based on my experience, a sprint review is rarely simple, and in fact, I consider it to be the most delicate session to facilitate.

The core issue is aligning the expectations of a disparate group of stakeholders outside of the team. These people are often more senior in the business relative to the team, they most certainly have less familiarity with the project compared to the team, and without wishing to generalize, they often have the attention span of a puppy with an attention-deficit disorder!

During Sprint Planning

Preparation for the sprint review actually starts during the previous sprint planning (see Figure 8.1). During the planning session, the team must ensure that tasks are being allocated appropriately in readiness for the sprint review. These tasks include

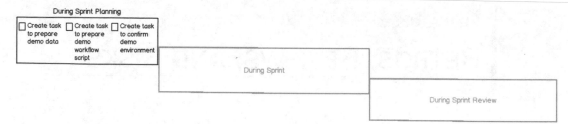

FIGURE 8.1   Preparation for the sprint review actually starts in the previous sprint planning session.

- Preparing some basic demo data

- Preparing a demo workflow script

- Ensuring the demo environment is working as expected

You don't want the team to spend too much time on these tasks, as the sprint review shouldn't be turned into a dog-and-pony show, but these tasks certainly need to be acknowledged.

There are also a few important points to stress to the team during sprint planning. First, the sprint review demo needs to be conducted on the staging environment rather than on the development server (and definitely not on an individual's machine). This is not a smoke-and-mirrors demonstration, and the team needs to really prove that what it has developed is releasable.

Second, although the team should feel relaxed during this session, it still needs to be taken seriously. During the sprint review, the efficacy of both the team and Scrum is on display to those who might not have had much exposure to either.

During the Sprint

Once into the sprint, the ScrumMaster and product owner need to start running through their collective checklist in anticipation of the review (see Figure 8.2). Items to cover off include location, invitations, painful attendees, presenters, and expectations.

Location

Confirm the location of the sprint review. Make sure that any relevant meeting rooms have been booked and that they are well equipped for the occasion. Double-check that a suitable projector, ample seating, network connectivity and a whiteboard are available. I also recommend testing that the equipment works as expected; nothing is more embarrassing than so-called technology experts unable to get the projector to work before the session even begins.

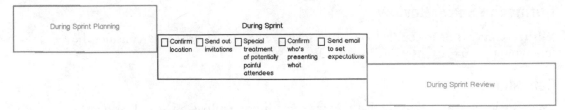

FIGURE 8.2   During the sprint, the ScrumMaster and product owner should go through their collective checklist in anticipation of the review.

Invitations

Ensure that invitations are sent to the relevant stakeholders as early as possible. In fact, there should be a standing invite to the regular attendees, so this suggestion applies only to any anomalous extras.

Painful Attendees

You may have concerns about a particular stakeholder who has a habit of taking center stage and issuing unwarranted criticism or off-tangent comments. If you have one of these delightful characters to deal with, I recommend that the ScrumMaster and/ or product owner visit him or her before the sprint review to present a sneak peak and to get some early input. People who feel a little bit special are less likely to be destructive during the review. We don't want to fix the results, but we certainly want to avoid unnecessary morale-busting reviews.

Presenters

Near the end of the sprint when you are able to ascertain exactly which user stories will likely be demonstrated, ensure that the team has decided who will be demonstrating what. It might be just one individual, or it could be a group effort—there is no hard and fast rule.

Expectations

Once the demonstrable stories have been determined, I recommend circulating an email to all attendees to give them a brief heads-up of what is going to be presented. The reason for doing so is that in the early sprint reviews of a project, the user-ready features with a snazzy UI are typically few and far between, which can lead to some miffed, eyebrow-raising stakeholders. For example, by informing them that the upcoming sprint review focuses primarily on the less visual, technical "plumbing," there is less likelihood of misaligning expectations.

This email also serves as a friendly reminder of when and where the session is with a gentle warning that any latecomers will have to supply coffee!

During the Sprint Review

When it comes time to conduct the actual sprint review (see Figure 8.3), consider the following tips to help ensure a smooth ride.

Refreshments

Everyone loves snacks. Ensure that there is something to nibble on as well as drinks (hard whiskey if you're really worried about how the review will go). I find it amusing that people's positive or negative judgment of a conference or training session often comes down to the catering, so don't forget to look after everyone's stomachs!

Scene Setting

Once everyone has settled in and engaged in some light banter over the refreshments, the product owner should briefly outline the sprint goal as well as reiterate what will be demonstrated. Also, for early sprints, it doesn't hurt to explain the definition of done (see Shortcut 11) to the stakeholders.

Impediments

Following the scene setting, it can also be a good idea to discuss any impediments that impacted the sprint, including why they occurred and how they were dealt with. This is an opportunity to lobby for greater assistance if there are any systemic impediments. An example might be the physical environment—perhaps a problem dealing with the facilities department in your mission to get larger desks or more breakout space.

In addition, I recommend using this segment to briefly make a point of key process improvements that were implemented to help achieve the sprint goal. Don't go into detail here, as this session is about reviewing the product, but a quick mention won't hurt and is a great opportunity to demonstrate to the stakeholders that the team is constantly improving.

The Main Event

Instead of a one-way showcase, the demo of the sprint's completed work should act as a prompt to encourage a two-way conversation between the business and the Scrum

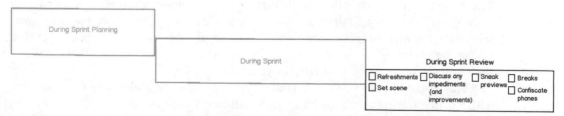

FIGURE 8.3   Some important points to remember during the sprint review.

team. It should be an open and honest discussion focusing on what was completed and what is coming up next.

Remember that this session should not become a smoke-and-mirrors slide show presentation to impress the attending stakeholders (unless, of course, your team is actually developing PowerPoint[1] or Keynote[2]!). I assure you that misleading demonstrations will only come back to bite the team.

Preview at the Review

It is a fundamental tenet that during the sprint review, the team should demonstrate only stories that meet the definition of done. It makes sense, but it can be very frustrating for some stakeholders, and the reality is that the team will possibly receive pressure to still show what has been worked on (even if it is not quite finished).

In this situation, instead of being a stubborn mule, I recommend creating an additional agenda item labeled "Coming Soon." This way, much like a movie preview, there is acknowledgment that the work isn't complete, yet the stakeholders still get a sense of work that's on the boiler and is coming soon to a sprint review near you!

Breaks and Phones

If your session is longer than an hour, I suggest taking 5 minute breaks every 45 minutes to maintain focus. But, be aware of the attention-deficit-disordered puppies who will get easily sidetracked and mugged in the corridors: don't let them stray far.

Also, although tough to enforce, try requesting that everyone submit their Black-Berrys[3] (providing that RIM is still around when this is published) at the door. The only problem is that you may need to hire armed guards to pry those smartphones out of stakeholders' hands! At the very least, you should announce at the start of the meeting, "For the safety of this sprint review, we request that you turn off all electrical devices." Good luck and at the very least, think up a creative punishment for those whose phones ring during the session.

So-Called Suggestions

There will no doubt be a range of questions and suggestions that surface throughout the session. I recommend that questions be controlled and kept on topic. The team should answer any and all questions that surface in relation to what is being demonstrated; however, questions that are tangential or completely off topic should be taken "offline" by the product owner and discussed with the relevant stakeholder(s) in a separate meeting.

---

1. To find out more about Microsoft PowerPoint, go to http://en.wikipedia.org/wiki/Microsoft_PowerPoint.
2. To find out more about Apple Keynote, go to http://en.wikipedia.org/wiki/Keynote_(presentation_software).
3. To find out more about BlackBerry, go to http://en.wikipedia.org/wiki/BlackBerry.

Acknowledge any suggestions made (no matter how outlandish they might sound) by writing them down on the whiteboard or index cards. With any luck, after seeing any crazy suggestions written in black and white, stakeholders will retract their pearls of wisdom. Any reasonable suggestions should of course be added to the product backlog (by the product owner) for further assessment and consideration.

Picnics or Battles

Sprint reviews can be akin to turning up for a summer picnic or, alternatively, turning up for pitched battle! It comes down to taking the necessary precautions and treating each session seriously while still having some fun. Don't assume that every stakeholder has the same level of background as the team, and ensure that all attendees are made to feel comfortable by always explaining what is happening and why.

Aligning everyone's expectations is the name of the game, and achieving this objective is critical if you prefer picnics to battles!

Shortcut 23: Retrospective Irrespective

Unfortunately, when a team is under pressure, the important sprint retrospective is often the first to get bumped until life is a bit more relaxed and under control. Even I have to admit that, in my earlier days as a ScrumMaster, I was guilty of skipping the retrospective on occasion. The irony is that this session is most valuable when the pressure is on and/or when things aren't running as expected. As such, discipline needs to be maintained, and the sprint retrospective should *always* remain a consistent event at the end of each sprint, irrespective of the noise surrounding it.

Reinforce Scrum's Values

It is important to remember Scrum's core values: *openness, courage, respect, focus,* and *commitment*. Nowhere should these values be applied more rigorously than in the sprint retrospective. Without an atmosphere of openness, you will never get to the heart of issues; without courage, the team won't be willing to confront problems head on; without respect, the team won't present criticism in a constructive fashion; and without focus and commitment, the team won't care enough to resolve the issues. Everyone should keep these values in mind at all times.

What If We're Running One-Week Sprints?

I've been asked before by teams who are running in very short, 1-week sprints whether they should perhaps run a retrospective only every two or three sprints (as opposed to on a weekly basis). Personally, I feel that 1-week sprints are too short (see Shortcut 8); however, if there is an insistence on shorter sprints, I don't recommend skipping the retrospective sessions. Instead, simply run shorter retrospectives but make sure that they still occur every sprint.

Location, Location, Location

To create an atmosphere of openness, the location where you hold your sprint retrospective is important. A large, stuffy boardroom with a long, impersonal mahogany table isn't conducive to the atmosphere you need and may turn your retrospective into more of an inquisition. Instead, I recommend a relaxed setting such as a coffee shop, a break room (if you have one), or even the kitchen area, which, because of its proximity to snacks and coffee, can be a great choice!

Getting Set

Ideally, you want your team arriving for the retrospective session prepared with a list of issues and suggestions so that you can get straight into it. To help facilitate this preparation, I recommend that you send an email before the session outlining potential areas to focus on. Examples of key areas include

- Communication
- Processes
- Scope
- Quality
- Environment
- Skills

Let's now explore a sample of some common improvement actions that might be triggered in each of these areas.

Communication

Communication areas include the following:

- Fixing disjointed communication between the product owner and development team (especially if the product owner isn't seated among the group).

- Removing disruptive and unnecessary communication between external stakeholders and the development team.

- Resolving dysfunctional communication within the team, typically due to an overreliance on written documentation (and email) rather than face-to-face discussion.

Processes

Process areas include the following:

- Upgrading software, hardware, and network connectivity.
- Confirming that the Scrum processes are well understood and clearly defined.
- Maintaining engineering standards relating to code quality, source control, and deployment processes.

Scope

Scope areas include the following:

- Making certain that significant changes to scope do not occur mid-sprint.
- Maintaining formatting consistency across all user story descriptions and acceptance criteria.
- Ensuring that the sprint planning scope is not ill-defined or too vague.

Quality

Quality areas include the following:

- Clearly defining and maintaining a consistent definition of done.
- Evolving test practices to enable more mature test automation.
- Ensuring that programmers are assuming ownership for the testing of their code and not leaving it totally up to the testers and/or product owner.

Environment

Environment areas include the following:

- Maintaining a collaborative environment that isn't too noisy and disruptive.
- Providing ample air-conditioning or heating.
- Making sure appropriate amenities are available (one microwave isn't going to cut it for 50 people!).
- Ensuring enough whiteboard space and other collaborative tools.

Skills

Skills areas include the following:

- Providing adequate training when new technologies are required.
- Conducting induction training for any new team members.
- Obtaining relevant specialist consulting when required.

Output of the Retrospective

When the juices start flowing, it isn't hard to generate a long list of issues to tackle. The trick is to not fall into the trap of getting overly keen and declaring that all issues will be resolved by the next retrospective! Instead, ensure that all improvement suggestions are documented, but aim to tackle no more than a few issues—perhaps one biggie and a couple of smaller ones. Nothing loses credibility faster than overpromising and underdelivering; so instead, do the opposite! Finally, write the agreed-upon actions on a large sheet of paper and place it near the task board as a constant reminder for the team. Please use discretion with this public display of action, as writing "Lock disruptive project sponsor in cage" and sticking it on the wall might not do much for your future job progression!

Format of the Retrospective

To keep things fresh, vary the format of the sprint retrospectives throughout the project. A number of approaches can be utilized, but for the sake of brevity, I focus on two of my favorites, nicknamed Circles and Bubbles.

Circles

The Circles technique employs an affinity mapping variation. For those unfamiliar with affinity mapping, it is essentially a graphical tool designed to amalgamate loose, unstructured ideas into collective groups.

Before reviewing the technique, let's identify the classic four questions often asked in Scrum retrospectives:

- What did we do well?
- What can we do better?
- What should we try next time?
- What issues do we need to escalate?

I prefer to simplify things even further by asking only two questions:

- What can we improve?
- What are we doing well?

Getting back to the technique, you first need to draw a horizontal scale on the whiteboard. On the very left write the label *Needs Improvement*; in the middle, jot down the more neutral *OK* label; and on the right, add the more encouraging *Going Well* label.

Now in keeping with the Scrum sticky-note tradition, hand each team member a bunch of sticky-notes and ask them to start writing their thoughts and/or issues on them. Once complete, direct the team to start sticking the notes on the wall, wherever along the scale they feel each note fits best. Be sure to time-box this step to avoid the dreaded analysis paralysis.

Once everyone places their notes on the board, it is time to align similar items to form groups. Next, use a nice thick marker (nonpermanent, or your issues will remain forever) to draw *circles* around the notes that reflect similar thoughts that are grouped closely together (see Figure 8.4); ignore the outliers for now. It will be rare for you not to identify a few common themes.

Once the groupings are completed, it is wise to briefly discuss any outliers with the team. More often than not, outliers result from misinterpretation or lack of understanding rather than from conflicting opinions.

Finally, as a team, address the circled groups in priority order (items further to the left will typically be of higher priority), and identify some actions to be followed up on in the forthcoming sprint to help address the improvement areas.

I like this approach for a few reasons:

- It avoids putting anyone on the spot (or in the spotlight).

- There is plenty of physical motion, which keeps the team alert and active.

- It is tactile and visual, which always makes life a bit more interesting.

- The team is able to immediately gauge the collective priorities by viewing the sticky-note groupings on the wall.

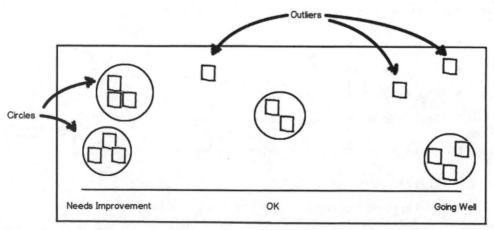

FIGURE 8.4   A Circles retrospective with similar suggestions grouped and circled.

Bubbles

The Bubbles technique is definitely my preferred approach for the first few retrospectives that you run with a freshly formed Scrum team (when the members haven't worked together before).

Bubbles works really well because it promotes immediate collaboration, helps everyone get to know one another in a noncontrived fashion, and again, doesn't put anyone on the spot.

So, how does it work? First, you need to come to the session prepared with paper and pen for everyone in the group.

This technique works best with an even number of team members, but you can easily make it work with uneven numbers. For demonstration purposes, let's say you have a team of eight.

The first step requires each person to document on paper the three most urgent issues that he or she feels should be focused on in the upcoming sprint. I recommend a 5-minute time-box for this step.

Next, get the individuals to pair up with a buddy (here you will obviously have four pairs, but there is no problem having groups of three instead if you have an uneven number). Again, during a 5-minute time-box, ask the pairs to decide, based on their combined lists, which three items should take priority overall.

You can probably see where this is heading by now, but in case you haven't guessed, the next step is to join two pairs together so that you now have two groups of four (see Figure 8.5). Once again, time-box this step, although you may offer a little

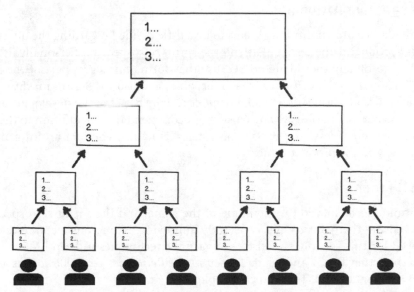

FIGURE 8.5 With this approach, the most urgent and important issues "bubble up" to the surface.

extra time because you now have groups of four debating the merits of their lists to determine the top three.

The penultimate step is to form a single group of eight to determine which three issues "bubble" right to the top of the top. By this stage, you should find that everyone's inhibitions have been dropped and that a healthy, open debate can now ensue, following which you will have determined what should be focused on next sprint.

Don't disregard all of the other valid suggestions that were uncovered in the earlier rounds of Bubbles. Instead, document them so that when you return for the subsequent retrospective, there is a healthy starting point to help get the ball rolling. Suggestions that were previously lower on the list may at a later stage become the top-priority focus points.

Finally, the team can rinse and repeat the same Bubbles activity to identify and acknowledge the successful behaviors and processes that the team wishes to explicitly keep active within the next sprint.

Seasoned Pros

When you are working with a truly battle-hardened group of Scrum aficionados, my advice is to forget about any formalized structure for your retrospective—it will just appear contrived. When a team is comfortable in its own skin, you will have no trouble getting the collective group to speak up and express their concern or joy with the status quo. Instead, simply go out for lunch or coffee with a pad and pen and shoot the breeze.

Retrospective Attendees

The broader Scrum community seems to be a little divided regarding the question of whether product owners should attend the sprint retrospective. Personally, I believe that they absolutely should attend because they form an integral part of the Scrum team. That being said, before your team becomes a well-oiled Scrum machine, there may be a few communication breakdowns, especially between the developers and the product owner. If you observe any tension, I recommend that in addition to the "official" retrospective session, the ScrumMaster should also conduct an informal one separately with the product owner.

Keep It Fresh

Inspection and adaptation is the name of the game, and the sprint retrospective is vital to ensure that your team is constantly improving. Numerous techniques can be employed for this session, so feel free to vary the techniques to keep life interesting and fresh. Esther Derby and Diana Larsen's *Agile Retrospectives* (2006) offers a whole host of different options that you can employ.

Most important, whatever happens, don't skip your retrospectives, irrespective of what is going on in the background!

Shortcut 24: Risk Takers and Mistake Makers

My mother is a retired kindergarten director without one iota of experience in the software world. That being said, she is a smart cookie with exceptional interpersonal skills, making her a fantastic educator. Now, while it would be a futile exercise discussing the technical elements of my profession (such as refactoring and code reviews) with my dear mom, I can certainly talk to her at length about the more communication-centric Scrum elements, such as sprint retrospectives and self-organizing teams.

I remember her reply when I was explaining some of the "revolutionary" ways that Scrum was assisting teams, such as the inclusion of frequent and open retrospectives. Her surprising response was, "What's the big deal? That just seems extremely obvious to me." At first I laughed at her apparently naïve comment, but after thinking about it further I realized that she was right! It absolutely should be obvious, so why isn't it? How come it is such a relatively new construct in our industry? After much thought, I concluded that the answer to that question comes down to one big ugly monster:

Fear!

It is no coincidence that one of Scrum's core values is courage. To successfully implement Scrum, we must overcome a range of fears. It is important to be fearful of fear (excuse the recursion), because it inevitably leads to diminished innovation, fosters a blame-game culture, and causes analysis paralysis when every action the team takes is scrutinized to avoid mistakes and the whipping stick that follows. With that scary prelude out of the way, let's tackle a selection of these common fears.

Fear of Change

This is a classic human phobia, and when we leap into Scrum from a more traditional approach, we make change in spades, don't we? How about programmers doing testing, releasable software every sprint, cross-functional and self-organizing teams, not to mention the lack of project managers, just to name a few—yikes!

So here's the thing: change is scary. It takes people out of their comfort zones, disrupts the status quo, and is often perceived as a threat to many who are comfortable with the present state. The sad reality is that there will always be those in any organization who will simply reject change irrespective of the expected benefits. It helps to understand and accept this organizational axiom, or you'll find yourself dwelling in a constant state of disappointment. I agree with Mike Cohn when he writes, "Rather than focusing on those who are reluctant or opposed to Scrum, spend your time and effort helping those who are already enthusiastic" (2009). I find that this is the best way to build the momentum needed to convince the naysayers.

Free to Change

A real key to initiating change is how the transition is framed and communicated. Not many folks are comfortable with forced or categorical change that completely readjusts the existing landscape. Instead, I recommend presenting the transition as an ongoing experiment. Communicate the fact that the change is under scrutiny rather than being a fait accompli, and if something doesn't work, the team will simply inspect and adapt together.

Understanding this failsafe option often allays the fears of those who are afraid to change.

Fear of Exposure

Some developers just like to be left alone in a corner to focus on their work (for better or worse) and can become quite defensive about perceived regular inspections of what they are working on. The problem for these closed-book developers is that Scrum is all about regular inspections—not to spy, of course, but to identify waste and misguided activity.

Inspection sessions such as the daily scrums, sprint reviews, and retrospectives may also uncover those individuals (and I use that word on purpose) who genuinely don't wish to do the right thing for the team. These few bad eggs are often the ones who are most afraid of exposure, fearing that the rug will be dramatically pulled out from under them and their poor-quality work will be discovered.

Free to Be Exposed

Growing up in Australia, we are taught very early on how dangerous sun exposure can be. Stay out too long, and you will be nursing red, painful skin for several days. That being said, let's not be too tough on our sunny source of life, as staying out for a short, disciplined period of time can lead to a nice, healthy glow and an important dose of vitamin D.

Scrum's focus on regular inspection of both the product and the process is all about gaining the glow and avoiding the burn. It is much easier to take care of tanned skin as opposed to red raw, burnt skin. This is exactly the same as in software development. If we detect issues early and often, there will be fewer painful surprises later on that require significant nursing and attention.

When inspections are framed in a positive way, team members (who genuinely wish to do the right thing) will embrace these sessions even if they have a natural inclination to stay in a corner with headphones on. And what about the bad eggs? Well, you will be able to find them nice and early so that they don't ruin everyone's breakfast!

Fear of Making Mistakes

Twisted organizations that have been warped and corrupted by a culture of finger-pointing, cover-ups, and internal conflict will have a very difficult time embracing Scrum or any other framework grounded in empirical process control. Scrum turns software development into an open book where mistakes are clearly visible.

The profound problem for these types of organizations is that the software industry (in particular) is a breeding ground for making mistakes because of the inherent risk surrounding developing software. Roman Pichler (2010) explains:

> Risk is therefore an intrinsic part of software development; no product can come to life risk-free. Correlated with risk is uncertainty. The more uncertainty there is, the riskier the project is. Uncertainty, in turn, is caused by a lack of knowledge. The less we know about what to develop and how to do it, the more uncertainty is present. Knowledge, uncertainty, and risk are therefore interlinked.

Free to Make Mistakes

The simple fact of the matter is that the greatest learning comes from taking risks and making mistakes. Don't believe me? Well, how about this example. Dan Senor and Saul Singer, authors of *Start-up Nation*, teach us about an aspect of Israel that is far more positive than the media images of constant conflict in its rough neighborhoods. The impressive revelation is that despite the ongoing constraints brought about by the constant threat of war and the fact that its population is a mere 7 million, it happens to have the highest number of technology start-ups in the world listed on the NASDAQ stock exchange (excluding only the United States and China). Senor and Singer (2009) offer some thoughts on why this might be the case:

> Israeli attitude and informality flow also from a cultural tolerance for what some Israelis call "constructive failures" or "intelligent failures." Most local investors believe that without tolerating a large number of these failures, it is impossible to achieve true innovation. In the Israeli military, there is a tendency to treat all performance—both successful and unsuccessful—in training and simulations, and sometimes even in battle, as value-neutral. So long as the risk was taken intelligently and not recklessly, there is something to be learned.

For me, this is a true lesson in macro-level agility, and it is reinforced by my own interactions with Americans and Israelis in the technology scene who certainly seem to have an amazingly high tolerance for so-called failure. As Asher Moses (2012) writes in the *Sydney Morning Herald*, "Over in Silicon Valley, failure is celebrated and seen as a chance to learn." We Aussies (among many others) can learn a lot from this positive attitude toward risk taking and mistake making.

I like the example set by software companies such as Facebook who often require developers to "push code to the live site within their first week" (Bosworth 2009).

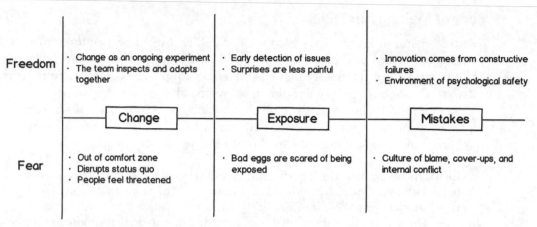

FIGURE 8.6   Whether it's change, exposure, or mistakes, for every fear there is also potential freedom from the fear.

This is smart psychology. It indicates to newbie team members that they are not going to achieve perfection immediately, that there is almost the expectation that a mistake could happen, and that it isn't a big deal. Getting the first mistake out of the way early and in a safe setting creates an environment of "psychological safety" (Cohn 2009). It generates comfort and a breeding ground for calculated risk and innovation.

Figure 8.6 offers a quick summary of these fears and how teams can become free of them.

Lighten the Mood

Nothing beats fear more than lightening the mood. In a particularly volatile pressure-cooker environment that I once worked in, we had a CEO who would tangibly relax a team following a costly mistake by announcing with a chuckle that, "It appears that the f**k-up-fairy has been to town again, doesn't it, people?" Although a little crude for some, this simple expression seemed to always relax the room before a solution was rapidly figured out.

Another beneficial side effect that you're likely to experience when openly discussing mistakes and vulnerabilities is the forging of closer bonds between team members. This openness helps to break down the artificial armor of perfection that many of us wear to hide the fact that we are human and fallible.

Finally, remember that every cloud has a silver lining. Those who are able to turn mistakes and problems into lessons and opportunities will soon find a working life totally free from fear.

Wrap Up

The three shortcuts in this chapter focused on a selection of tactics, tools, and tips to help your team make the most of their sprint reviews and retrospectives. Let's recap what was covered:

Shortcut 22: To-Dos for Your Sprint Reviews

- How to effectively prepare for the upcoming sprint review

- The importance of not turning the sprint review into a one-way demonstration

- Elements to consider incorporating in the sprint review

Shortcut 23: Retrospective Irrespective

- The importance of never skipping a sprint retrospective

- Two useful retrospective formats: Bubbles and Circles

- Key improvement areas to inspect and adapt

Shortcut 24: Risk Takers and Mistake Makers

- The importance of establishing a failsafe environment to ensure open and honest feedback sessions

- Common fears that burden teams

- A selection of measures to help teams overcome these fears

Chapter 9
MANAGING THE MANAGERS

Even though the Scrum framework doesn't explicitly call out the specific involvement and contribution of senior stakeholders, project sponsors, and other managers, it certainly doesn't imply that these roles don't exist or that they're not integral to the success of our projects.

The following three shortcuts offer a range of options for integrating these senior, high-level roles into the Scrum landscape.

Shortcut 25: Perception Is Reality focuses on managing the perceptions of project sponsors who may be unfamiliar with Scrum. Shortcut 26: Our Lords and Masters suggests an option for aligning multiple ScrumMasters in larger organizations through the proposed Chief ScrumMaster role. Finally, Shortcut 27: Morphing Managers in the Matrix details the efficacy of creating and maintaining a team-centric organizational structure and discusses how project managers and functional managers can still work with Scrum teams.

Shortcut 25: Perception Is Reality

We play card games during our estimation sessions, we decorate our areas with colorful sticky notes, we don't rush around like panicked turkeys at Christmas, we get together in a daily huddle and have a laugh at some poor developer wearing the broken-build cowboy hat (see Shortcut 20) —hmm, sounds a lot like . . . oh, don't say it . . . *FUN!*

Now, although Scrum officially prescribes only three roles—the ScrumMaster, product owner, and development team—if you want your Scrum projects to succeed, you had best learn fast how to get on with another important role that is financially critical to most projects—the project sponsor.

Sadly, many of you will have worked with project sponsors (especially from a non-software background) who are convinced that an axiom of office life is that productivity is mutually exclusive to having some fun.

Without wishing to overgeneralize, if one (or more) of your sponsors has a background in an industry synonymous with a command-control culture they will likely feel that working 18-hour days is a cultural norm and that if you don't look like you're about to have your fourth coronary, then you're simply not focused enough! Based on that premise, imagine how they feel about seeing people leave work at a reasonable and consistent time, hearing constant chit-chat between previously disparate teams, and watching teams spend time on so-called non-functional work, such as unit testing and refactoring. I'll tell you what they will be feeling—discomfort at best and fury at worst!

Even though the product owner should be the primary interface between the Scrum team and the more senior project sponsor, you have a role as the ScrumMaster to keep the sponsor from blowing a gasket. You must use your powers of persuasion to constantly align expectations by understanding the sponsor's perspective and reconciling it with that of the team.

Build a Relationship

Don't just wait for the more official sprint review or worse, an emergency, to meet with the sponsor. Instead, be proactive and set up a regular update session irrespective of what is happening—perhaps catch up for lunch or set up a regular coffee outing with the sponsor. During these regular sessions, you can reinforce the positive changes that are occurring while also gauging the sponsor's current perception of how the project is going.

Corporate politics can be one of the trickiest and most persistent impediments facing your teams, so having a strong relationship with the sponsor offers you a chance to potentially obtain both direct and indirect clues regarding any politics that might be a hurdle down the track. With this insight, you can start planning how to deal with it if or when the time comes.

Reference Point

It is always a good idea to have a firm and unambiguous understanding of the overall goal of the project. Sure, as far as Scrum is concerned, this perception is the product owner's responsibility; however, it is wise to ensure that the sponsor has plenty of input into the product's high-level overview that forms the guiding beacon from beginning to end.

To create the high-level overview, I recommend the use of a simple product "one-pager." Table 9.1 presents an example (inspired by Jim Highsmith and Pete Deemer).

While the sponsor may be unfamiliar with the details of the emerging product backlog, he or she should be completely comfortable with the overview presented in the one-pager. Contention that potentially arises down the track with any of the specific requirements should ultimately be resolved by the solution that best aligns with what has been captured in this artifact.

Involve Them

I find that sponsors become less upset when confronted with problems if they are involved in the resolution. So, be proactive when an issue arises—approach them with a range of options and make them feel involved in determining the remedial course of action.

TABLE 9.1   A Simple One-Page Product Overview

Elevator Pitch:	For...Who...That...Unlike...
Target Customers:	1) People who work in... 2) Those who need a... 3) ...
Major Capabilities:	1) Share content with... 2) Personalize ads on... 3) ...
Benefits / Differentiation:	1) More accurate than... 2) Better integration with... 3) ...
Metrics / Goals:	1) X users per month 2) Y click-through-rate per month 3) ...
Major Milestones:	1) v1.0 alpha 2) v1.0 beta 3)...
Performance Attributes:	1) X requests per second 2) Y concurrent users 3) ...
Trade-off Options:	Scope: Flexible Resources: Fixed Schedule: Firm

Also, I like to occasionally send out a special guest invite to a Planning Poker session (see Shortcut 14). These estimation workshops are dynamic, collaborative, and informative and, if facilitated well, will leave the sponsor feeling that the team certainly knows what it's talking about!

Finally, it goes without saying that you should invite and involve the sponsors in the regular sprint review during which they get an opportunity to give the team feedback and offer encouragement (see Shortcut 22).

Keep Them in the Loop

Sponsors hate to be kept in the dark. Thanks to Scrum's strong emphasis on transparency and visibility, there should no longer be any deep, dark secrets. Embrace this

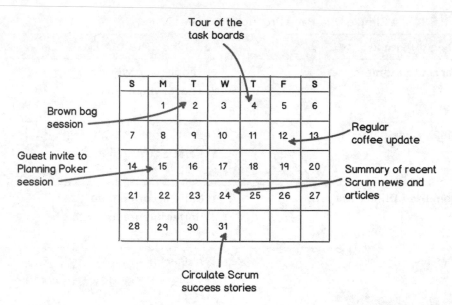

FIGURE 9.1   Maintain multiple touch points with your project sponsors to keep them in the loop.

facet of Scrum by filling up your monthly calendar (see Figure 9.1) with a selection of the following options:

- Take the sponsor on a "Tour of the Task Boards" now and again. Explain what all the colorful sticky-notes mean and why you had that strange little spike in the burndown chart earlier in the week (see Shortcut 21).

- Conduct regular presentations or "brown-bag" sessions that delve into specific Scrum practices, such as Explaining Relative Estimation or Understanding User Stories.

- Circulate books and articles to reinforce the popularity of Scrum. Conservative organizations often don't like feeling that they are pioneering new ways of working, so emphasizing that Scrum is fast becoming more mainstream is often very reassuring to them.

- Promote your successes by circulating a monthly Scrum Success Stories update. It doesn't need to simply focus on quantitative measures, such as reduced bug counts or faster deployment times; it should also be used to promote the more qualitative benefits. Achievements, such as the breaking down of walls between previously siloed-off groups are certainly causes for celebration.

- I'm a big fan of sharing experiential war stories. Mike Cohn (2009) refers to these as "internal experience report presentations" and correctly points out that "nothing beats hearing from someone who is already doing it."

Maintain Diplomatic Discipline

Never say no is a lesson that I have learned over time. No one likes being told no, so we often need to play some games to disguise this message.

Suddenly behaving like an aggressive rottweiler that feels empowered to push back and say no under the "protection" of the Scrum rules is never a good idea. Even if the sponsor understands and appreciates the principles behind the pushback, human nature dictates that no one likes to be told a categorical NO. The sponsors will push back if they feel that they have been curtly disregarded.

I personally like to use a simple approach when saying no. This is how it goes:

Sponsor: "I know that we're now well into the sprint, but can we please briefly postpone user story ABC and implement user story XYZ instead?"

Me: "Sure thing, Mr. Stakeholder, we can do anything. However, please take into account the implications of enacting this change. Some of these implications include disrupting our strong momentum, calling for a sprint cancellation, and worst of all, undermining our Scrum process and damaging the faith that the developers have in the new and positive way that we're working.

Would you agree with me that the implications at this point outweigh the benefits? So, how about we tackle user story XYZ first thing in the next sprint, which starts in a few short days?"

I find that more often than not, this approach works wonders and really generates a win-win situation: everyone goes away getting what they want while also feeling that they have been magnanimous and reasonable.

You also have potential for pushback when you start discussing the fact that time should be dedicated to pure technical tasks (as opposed to functional tasks), such as unit testing and refactoring. I find the easiest way to tackle these issues is to use statistics and precedents from other well-known and highly successful companies. For example, when I explain the need to pay off accruing technical debt, I like to talk the sponsor's language and quote from a *Wall Street Journal* article about eBay:

eBay's system, which involved 25 million lines of inflexible code, soon became a liability. . . .The benefits are fuzzy and the risks are very real. Yet you have to do it. If you don't, you fall behind and you go out of business. (Fowler and Morrison 2010)

While the sponsor may not truly understand what technical debt and refactoring is, I have found the "If it's good enough for eBay and it's in the *Wall Street Journal*, then we should probably do it as well" attitude to be prevalent and that suits me just fine.

Remember Who Pays the Bills

Remember the expression, He (or she) who has the gold, makes the rules? So, the sponsors—the ones paying for what the Scrum team is developing—have the right and ability to run things however they like. Beware, that perception is reality. The last thing that you want is to revert to the dark old days simply because the sponsor doesn't understand Scrum.

If there is a perception that Scrum is creating teams of ill-disciplined cowboys, then your job, should you choose to accept it, is to work with the sponsor to foster a stronger, deeper understanding of why Scrum is beneficial and how it offers the best possible chance of getting them the best bang for their buck.

Shortcut 26: Our Lords and Masters

When one ScrumMaster turns into two, then three, then four, life begins to gets more exciting. Scrum has clearly taken a stronghold in your organization and is settling in for the long haul.

Although this is a great situation, care must be taken to erect strong scaffolding to help guide the positive surge as well as to maintain a level of consistency and discipline across the expanding groups.

To ensure that problems don't arise, consider the creation of a new position complete with a fresh remit to maintain standards and consistency. The Scrum equivalent of a PMO (project management office) would be ideal. However, setting up a PMO is no easy feat, and because this book is about identifying effective shortcuts, I recommend a simpler alternative (at least to start with): the creation of the Chief Scrum-Master position.

ScrumMaster versus Chief ScrumMaster

Although Scrum doesn't prescribe any functional lead roles, the reality is that there needs to be a person who handles the responsibilities, such as HR, career progression, and technical mentoring, for the various functions. Simply put, the Chief ScrumMaster performs this role for a group of ScrumMasters and also acts as the organization-wide strategic Scrum coach (see Figure 9.2). If you prefer a looser structure, then you could instead view the Chief ScrumMaster as the facilitator of the ScrumMaster Community of Practice (see Shortcut 27).

Now that the general relationship between the two roles has been established, let's explore the specific functions of each, starting with the new Chief ScrumMaster role.

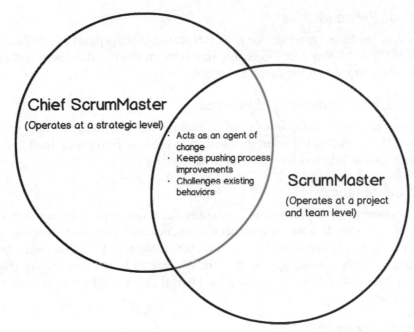

FIGURE 9.2 While the roles are different, they share important commonalities.

Core Functions of the Chief ScrumMaster

Cohn's *Succeeding with Agile* (2009) provides an excellent basis for the core functions of a Scrum-based PMO, and I'm going to start with a selection of these functions for our Chief ScrumMaster position description. I have put my own spin on these descriptions, so for Cohn's original descriptions, please refer to his book.

Training and Coaching

Novice ScrumMasters need to learn how to become good ScrumMasters, and maturing ScrumMasters need to learn how to become great ScrumMasters. Programs need to be created to facilitate this education process.

Challenge Existing Behaviors

Cohn (2009) talks about challenging the teams "who are falling back into old habits." This is obviously important, but in the case of the Chief ScrumMaster, it is also critical to continually challenge the *organization* (on a whole) if it slips back into its more systemic bad habits.

Provide and Maintain Tools

Whether the business decides to use high-tech or low-tech tools (or a combination of both), the various artifact templates need to be defined, adapted, and version controlled.

Define and Refine Metrics

Metrics should be used carefully for good rather than evil purposes (see Shortcut 19). The Chief ScrumMaster needs to ensure that relevant metrics have been formulated and are being utilized for the correct purpose.

Help Establish Communities of Practice

Function-specific communities of practice should ideally form organically from the grassroots (Cohn 2009). However, they will often need the initial kick-start and occasional shot-in-the-arm to keep them running effectively.

Ensure Consistency

Ensuring consistency across teams is possibly the most important function of the Chief ScrumMaster. It is important that consistency and discipline are maintained, especially when there are multiple teams and ScrumMasters. If certain teams need or would like to apply varying approaches (for whatever reason), then these variations should be adopted in a systematic and purposeful fashion with guidance from the Chief ScrumMaster.

Coordinate Teams

With multiple interdependent teams working on the same product backlog, processes need to be defined and maintained to ensure coordination occurs as seamlessly as possible.

In Addition . . .

The following are some additional functions that I feel can be added to Cohn's list.

Ongoing Scrum Promotion

Promoting Scrum should occur not only in the early stages of the adoption but also as the organization evolves. New stakeholders will be regularly coming on board, and they will need to understand the incumbent Scrum environment.

Developing the Approach

Remember that Scrum is a framework and not a prescribed method (see Shortcut 2). Therefore, the specific, fit-for-purpose approach for an organization should be initially defined by the Chief ScrumMaster.

Company-Level Education

As each new Scrum initiative or practice gets introduced for the first time, the business needs ongoing education to ensure that the proposed benefits are understood.

Aligning the Teams' Definitions of Done

Coordinating the defining and evolution of a consistent definition of done across all teams is important to ensure that expectations are aligned, especially during key integration periods.

Continual Process Improvement via Collective Retrospectives

Many useful suggestions will bubble up from the various team sprint retrospectives, and it is important that any golden ideas that Team X comes up with (that other teams may also find helpful) are leveraged across all groups.

Impediment Escalation

Not all impediments that disrupt an individual team can be resolved by the individual ScrumMaster, especially issues relating to organizational constraints, such as the physical working environment and/or incentive schemes. The Chief ScrumMaster should be the first escalation point for such impediments.

HR for the ScrumMasters

Just like everyone else in the organization, ScrumMasters have HR requirements that need to be managed, such as career planning, remuneration reviews, training, and mentoring.

Creating a Physical Environment Conducive to Scrum

To work successfully, Scrum needs to exist in a collaborative and comfortable team environment with minimal disruptions from the outside world (see Shortcut 3). Ensuring a close working relationship with the facilities department who can assist to modify the workplace where and when required is integral to Scrum's success.

Core Functions of the ScrumMaster Role

When the ScrumMaster is a lone wolf in a small organization, then the Chief Scrum-Master functions listed earlier will also need to taken on by the ScrumMaster. However, when there is the luxury of a Chief ScrumMaster, the ScrumMaster should then be free to focus primarily on the following roles and responsibilities.

Process Improvement

Identifying key improvement points with help from quantitative metrics (see Shortcut 19) as well as through the more qualitative sprint retrospectives (see Shortcut 23) is a fundamental responsibility of the ScrumMaster.

Impediment Management

One of the most publicized of all ScrumMaster functions is the controlling of impediments to ensure that project speed bumps don't turn into brick walls (see Shortcut 9).

Diplomacy

Especially in the early days, silos will likely exist between the various groups who are required to work together in a new Scrum team. Bringing these groups together around the campfire is one of the more subtle, yet critical, responsibilities of the ScrumMaster.

Coaching

It is imperative that the ScrumMaster comprehensively understands the broader Scrum framework, and more specifically, he or she needs to be highly proficient with the approaches adopted among the teams. This includes being an expert with the various tools and techniques being used.

Managing Change

Regular changes will be made to overall product scope as well as individual product backlog items. Controlling these changes and guiding the various parties in managing the changes is extremely important.

Maintaining the Definition of Done

Once the definition of done has been defined by the Scrum team (see Shortcut 11), the ScrumMaster needs to work hand in glove with the product owner and developers to ensure that it is maintained.

Maintaining Effective Communication

Scrum relies on positive human interaction; therefore, the ScrumMaster needs to actively encourage a culture that allows such interaction to occur.

Updating Artifacts

The ScrumMaster needs to work with the developers to ensure that sprint artifacts are regularly updated (which often requires perfecting the art of chasing without nagging).

Facilitating Workshops

Prior to a project kicking off, the ScrumMaster needs to work with the product owner to facilitate the creation of the product backlog by conducting user story workshops and estimation sessions (see Shortcut 14).

Facilitating Scrum Activities

Several activities occur throughout the sprint iteration, and the ScrumMaster is responsible for their running smoothly. This includes managing the logistics and facilitation of the following:

- Daily scrums (see Shortcut 20)

- Sprint planning (see Shortcut 8)

- Sprint reviews (see Shortcut 22)

- Sprint retrospectives (see Shortcut 23)

A motivated ScrumMaster will also make efforts to constantly spice up these sessions by introducing various formats and locations to keep life interesting.

A Consistent Ecosystem

Phew! When you read these lists of functions, you can begin to really appreciate that maintaining a successful Scrum ecosystem is no trivial matter.

I believe that the key to success, especially as the broader Scrum rollout gains momentum, is maintaining a level of consistency, discipline, and continual education. A centralized Chief ScrumMaster, supported by dedicated ScrumMasters, will ensure that these critical success factors are achieved.

Shortcut 27: Morphing Managers in the Matrix

It's no secret why it took electric-powered cars so long to come about. Powerful incumbents, satisfied with the status quo, are more than willing to completely repress any movement for overall positive change and efficiency. You can't really blame them—it's a survival game whereby one industry becomes obsolete to establish a newer and more efficient one. This is the same difficult battle that we face when trying to introduce Scrum broadly across a large organization that is not receptive to change. Many Scrum adoptions (particularly in larger, more traditional companies) require the typical hierarchical power centers to evolve (or potentially even disappear), and to accomplish this evolution requires visionary leadership that is genuinely interested in encouraging continuous improvement as opposed to playing politics.

This shortcut explores some possible options to help organizations that are stuck in their traditional structural backwaters. This is obviously a big, deep topic to cover in a shortcut, but let's be ambitious! Specifically, we will focus on three key areas: (1) options for the general organizational structure; (2) options for the traditional project manager, and (3) options for the functional managers.

Evolving Out of the Matrix

With increasing emphasis on project-related work, organizational structures have had to adapt. The most recent mainstream evolution was the movement in many organizations toward more project-centric structures, such as the balanced matrix. The question, though, is whether they have evolved enough to generate a sustainable, conducive environment for Scrum projects to successfully operate. Before answering that, let's briefly recap some of the basic characteristics of typical organizational structures.

Functional Organizations

Characteristics of functional organizations include the following:

- Made up of specialized departments.
- Functional managers have ultimate authority (see Figure 9.3).

Projectized Organizations

Characteristics of projectized organizations include the following:

- Made up of dynamically generated project teams.
- Project managers have ultimate authority (see Figure 9.4).

Balanced Matrix Organizations

Characteristics of balanced matrix organizations include the following:

- Made up of vertical specialized departments and horizontal project teams.
- Authority (supposedly) balanced between project managers and functional managers (see Figure 9.5).

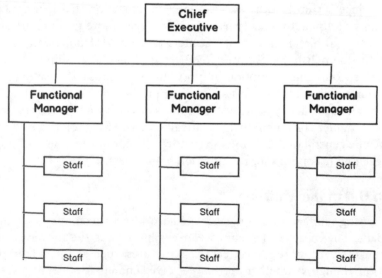

FIGURE 9.3   A typical functional organization chart.

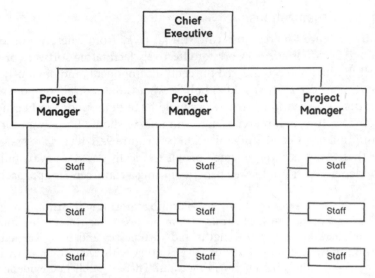

FIGURE 9.4 A typical projectized organization chart.

Alignment with the balanced matrix structure is becoming increasingly common in large organizations. In this structure, projects are run by project managers who are temporarily assigned people (and other resources) from the various functional managers for the duration of the project. Once the project is done and dusted, the project team disbands and everyone returns to their functional, operational roles or moves onto another project team. To many nonagilists, this setup is the perfect happy medium.

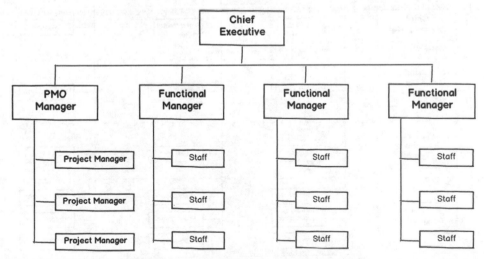

FIGURE 9.5 A typical balanced matrix organization chart.

Team-Centric Organizations

So why is the balanced matrix structure still far away from where we need it to be? Well, although Scrum is a framework for effectively facilitating software projects, the project itself should not be considered the central component (and obviously the functional departments certainly shouldn't be). So what is the central component that the next-generation organizational structure should be built around? I'm hoping that the answer is obvious to you; however, if not, your answer should be . . . wait for it . . . the Scrum team! In a team-centric organization (see Figure 9.6), teams are assigned projects rather than projects being assigned people (typically based on availability). Agile coach Rob Maher points out the key benefit of using a team-centric approach:

> Teams go through a proven lifecycle—Forming, Storming, Norming, and Performing (Tuckman, 2010). This maturation process takes time, often months. Team members know their strengths and weaknesses and have learned how to communicate, collaborate and resolve conflict with each other. Why break up what has become a high performing team? There is published evidence that short-lived groups of people brought together for a project are correlated with lower productivity. (Maher 2011)

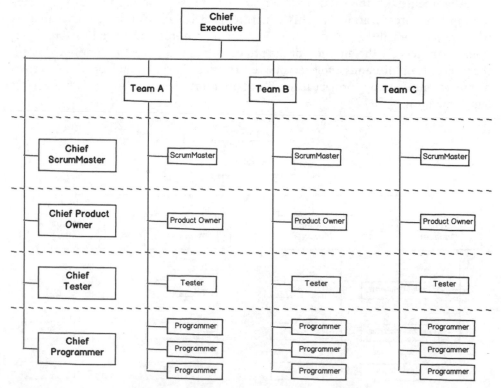

FIGURE 9.6   The most Scrum conducive organizational structure.

Apart from the fundamental benefit of higher productivity, there are other advantages to the team-centric approach, such as the ability to provide more accurate forecasts because of the longer-running historical velocity data that a jelled Scrum team has managed to accumulate (see Shortcut 19).

Think about a team-centric structure as similar to the cross-functional commando units in the military. Instead of forming new units when a mission arises, the most suitable preexisting units get assigned the missions that they are best able to take on. Sure, there may be the odd situation where the commando unit needs to add another type of specialist, but the vast bulk of the unit always stays together because of their strong cohesiveness, trust, and operational familiarity.

Project Managers Aren't Disappearing

Scrum describes only three roles: the ScrumMaster, the product owner, and the development team. This seemingly simplistic breakdown inevitably leads to the same awkward questions from incumbent project managers time after time: "Umm, so what happens to us project managers?" The tough love response is offered by Cohn (2009) when he states, "In Scrum we recognize the untenable role of the project manager and eliminate it." This leads to the next question (usually asked in panicked tones): "So what happens to all of the crucial project management functions, such as scheduling, budgeting, and planning?" I answer this question with something like, "Well, actually, those responsibilities are split among the three different Scrum roles to varying degrees." The project manager, now reaching for a respirator, continues with, "So . . . what does that mean for me?" I'll then respond sensitively with, "Well, it means that if you want to play in the Scrum world, then you'll have to transition to become either a ScrumMaster, product owner, or developer—it's pretty simple." Now despondent, the project manager will often sigh and offer a final claim along the lines of, "I like the sound of Scrum, but I love being a project manager and don't think that I want to give it up, so I guess no Scrum for me."

I've seen this happen and I don't much like it. Throwing the baby out with the bathwater is wasteful, so is there another option to involve more traditional project managers in Scrum projects? My opinion is yes (with a big *but*). The *but* is that I totally agree that there is no place for a traditional project manager in a single Scrum team. Where I see the potential for the reintroduction of project managers is when the development efforts utilizing Scrum are considered to be part of a larger multidepartment project. Let's explore this further.

The Project Big Picture

More often than not, Scrum development projects don't just operate in an organizational vacuum. At the tail end of development, there is typically a flurry of activity occurring in other parts of the organization. The marketing team is trying to understand how to best position the new product, the sales team is trying to understand the product for demonstrations, the customer service team is skilling up to handle customer queries, and the finance team needs to integrate the new pricing and revenue models based on the new offering (Figure 9.7). Wow! There sure is a lot to coordinate and manage here. I personally feel that the intra-organizational coordination, logistical planning, scheduling, and tracking are massive roles and ones that are nicely suited to the traditional project manager.

Third Parties

Kenneth Rubin (2012) offers another suggestion as to where the project manager can add value—the coordination of efforts between the Scrum team(s) and contractors who might not be using Scrum.

> A project manager can also be helpful on development efforts where using Scrum represents just one small part of a much greater product or services development. For example, there might be subcontractors, internal non-Scrum teams, and other internal organizations associated with delivering the product.

The Future of Functional Managers

Now that we've looked at some options for the project manager, let's change paths and focus on what opportunities there are for functional managers as Scrum enters the fold.

Here's the problem: a great developer has been promoted to the role of functional manager. This position bestows hierarchical privilege that the new manager comes to

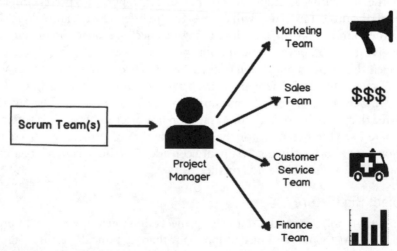

FIGURE 9.7 The project manager can be an important interface between the Scrum team(s) and the other departments.

enjoy and value. Sure, they may no longer be working hands-on in the code as much as they would like and instead are spending more time in boring meetings, delegating tasks, and fiddling with administrative paperwork, but hey, being able to tell their mom that they're now in a management role is pretty cool, right?

The issue is that in Scrum, there is no prescribed functional manager who needs to delegate work to the self-organizing teams. These functional managers are then left wondering what becomes of them. Do they now get stripped of their title thanks to Scrum?

Well, I don't believe so. My solution to the problem is to simply help them redefine what it means to be a functional manager. The first thing that I typically say to them is similar to what Scrum trainer and Stormglass CEO Pete Deemer (2011) recommends when he suggests, "In simplest terms, the manager in Scrum is less of a 'nanny' to the Team and more of a mentor or 'guru,' helping them learn, grow and perform." *Usually no arguments so far from the incumbent functional manager.*

Next, I talk about the fact that with multiple Scrum teams, there is a strong need to help ensure that technical standards have been defined and that someone is able to guide the team to resolve technical impediments both intra- and inter-team. *Our functional manager is still happy.*

Moving on, I discuss the need for someone to be able to identify the knowledge gaps so that the applicable learning and development programs can be evolved—on both the technical and domain levels. *No objections yet.*

I continue by mentioning that we also need someone capable and qualified to help recruit new developer talent when we form new teams or need to replace someone. *Still no objections.*

Finally, I tell the functional managers that they can throw those painful delegation tasks that they are "forced" to do out the window so that they can get back to focusing on what they really love to do! Typical response to this redefinition: *"Sounds super sweet! When do we start?"*

I see this structural shift as a move away from hierarchical commanding and a step toward "community of practice" facilitation. If this transition occurs successfully, then I really don't mind if they wish to hang on to their functional manager titles.

Let's Be Realistic

Just because Scrum describes only three roles, it shouldn't mean that all others are rendered superfluous or redundant. The changing of organizational structure and the wholesale removal of traditional functions, such as the project manager, is not only unrealistic but in many cases unnecessary. Thinking with an open mind can uncover options whereby these traditional roles may be repurposed without corrupting the true Scrum model.

By embracing existing functions, such as higher-level project management, we may be able to knock down a considerable barrier blocking the introduction of Scrum, especially in larger, more traditional organizations.

Wrap Up

The three shortcuts included in this chapter focused on a selection of tactics, tools, and tips to integrate senior stakeholders into the Scrum landscape. Let's recap what was covered:

Shortcut 25: Perception Is Reality

- The importance of establishing a fluid working relationship with the project sponsor(s)

- A helpful approach for generating the product vision: the one-pager

- Tips for ensuring that project sponsors continue to feel included and kept in the loop

Shortcut 26: Our Lords and Masters

- Differentiating between the role of the ScrumMaster and that of the Chief ScrumMaster

- Understanding the core functions of the Chief ScrumMaster

- Understanding the core functions of the ScrumMaster

Shortcut 27: Morphing Managers in the Matrix

- Why a team-centric organizational structure is preferable to the typical balanced matrix or functional models

- Potential options for traditional project managers who don't wish to transition into one of the core Scrum roles

- The evolution of the functional manager role

Chapter 10

LARGER LESSONS

When you're working hard and sprinting away, it can sometimes be very difficult to see the wood from the trees. To finish up, in this final chapter we're going to take a step back and look at the bigger picture to fully appreciate what is truly important at the end of the day.

The following three shortcuts provide the final three larger lessons. Shortcut 28: Scrum Rollout Reckoning examines a selection of "macro" metrics focusing on ways to measure your organization's evolving Scrum and agile abilities. Shortcut 29: Eyes on the Prize delves into the importance of self-organization for unleashing your team's full potential. Finally, Shortcut 30: Shortcut to the Final Level shines the spotlight on three immensely powerful and fundamental words: *transparency, inspection*, and *adaptation*.

Shortcut 28: Scrum Rollout Reckoning

If you read Shortcut 19, then as promised, here is part two. If you didn't, don't worry because I am sticking to my earlier assertion that you can read these shortcuts independently, but hey, it doesn't hurt to promote another handy shortcut, now, does it? Anyway, the big difference between this shortcut and Metrics that Matter is that now we are ready to move up a level and discuss metrics from a more holistic Scrum rollout perspective rather than at a Scrum project level. The same core advice still applies, such as the need to use metrics for good and not for evil purposes, which we explore shortly.

How Agile Are We?

I sometimes hear industry colleagues comment that their project team is "about 85 percent agile," or they might say something like, "We are using Scrum to about 50 percent capacity." The typical question that goes through my head when I hear comments such as these is, "What the hell does *that* mean?"

Let's take a look at the first point: "We're 85 percent agile." Really? So, does that mean that if you do things a little bit differently, perhaps start implementing a few more practices, then you will soon be 100 percent agile? Wow, you can't do any better than 100 percent, so when you hit this auspicious milestone, then I suppose there is nothing more to do except maintain what you're doing, right? Wrong! I've said it before, but you shouldn't need me to convince you that 100 percent agile perfection is never attainable! There is always something that can be done better, and considering that Scrum is fundamentally about continuous improvement, how can perfection ever be achieved? Classifying your agility in terms of percentages just doesn't make sense.

I will answer the second point (using Scrum to 50 percent capacity) more succinctly—you are either doing Scrum or not. It is binary (see Figure 10.1). Implementing partial Scrum was discussed in Shortcut 2 via a comparison to chess—you can't play without all the pieces. In the same way, you can't be doing 50 percent Scrum—if you are then you might be doing something that resembles Scrum, but it sure isn't Scrum.

Humans Love to Measure

The obsession with measurement possibly starts for us when that first pencil mark is drawn on the wall by our proud parents measuring how tall we're growing. Humans love to score and we love to assess our progress for a multitude of reasons. This isn't a bad thing if done for the right reasons, such as gauging continual process and measuring what Scrum was able to deliver (especially relative to the initial potential benefits laid out in Shortcut 1). Assessment can also be a great team motivator to give everyone a sense of forward motion and progress in the same way that a belt system works in martial arts. Sure, to some, the belt is more important than the art; however, to most, the belt indicates that they have improved and been recognized for their hard work, and that isn't a bad thing in my book.

There are two primary reasons that you might find it necessary to quantify the success of your Scrum rollout:

- To decide whether you should continue with Scrum.

- To assess your team's progress along their Scrum journey.

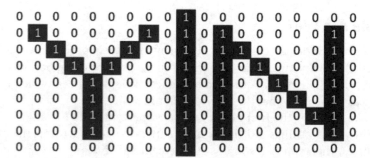

FIGURE 10.1 Practicing Scrum is binary—you're either doing Scrum or you're not—there is no partial Scrum.

Should We Continue?

How do you gauge whether your initial Scrum rollout has been successful? Well, you could rely on a bunch of numbers on a spreadsheet comparing your pre- and post-Scrum projects, but I for one don't like using this approach (at least not in isolation), primarily because Scrum is not a mechanical process. It is so reliant on people and culture that even with fantastic quantitative results, the introduction of Scrum may have caused such upheaval that too many people are unhappy and that is not good for Scrum's long-term survival.

An approach I particularly like that helps to enrich any quantitative feedback is a simple, subjective, collaborative survey that I first read about in Scrum trainer Gabrielle Benefield's paper (2008). To gauge the effectiveness of their pioneering global Scrum rollout at Yahoo!, Benefield and Deemer used a simple survey based on the following six criteria:

- How much the team got done in 30 days
- Clarity of goals—what the team was supposed to deliver
- Collaboration and cooperation within the team
- Business value of what the team produced in 30 days
- Amount of time wasted, work thrown out, cycles misused
- Overall quality and "rightness" of what the team produced

Everyone involved in the survey had the opportunity to match the criteria to the following possible responses:

- Scrum much worse
- Scrum worse
- Scrum about the same
- Scrum better
- Scrum much better

The aggregation of these results told a distinct and positive story about Scrum's efficacy as perceived by the collective.

Costs versus Benefits

Now, irrespective of all of the warm, fuzzy results you hopefully obtain from your surveys, they shouldn't be the only indicator of whether Scrum is going to be a raging success across your entire organization. Remember that, unlike an isolated pilot project, Scrum in the broader organizational context doesn't operate in a vacuum. Transitioning from a controlled trial to a broad adoption introduces a range of new and often significant impediments that must now be considered. These impediments may include collocating cross-functional teams, modifying incentive schemes, adjusting the office layout, and overhauling sign-off procedures and client contract structures—just to name a few.

The cold, hard reality is that in some organizations, the initial Scrum rollout may serve only to identify the various environmental and cultural constraints that will impede the successful implementation of Scrum. The organization simply may not be ready, willing, or able to remove the necessary constraints.

Are We Getting Better?

Back to more positive news. Let's say that Scrum is alive and thriving in your organization. It is only natural, then, to want to gauge whether you are stagnating or progressing.

To make this assessment, you need a relative benchmark that is pegged to either your past performance or your performance relative to others (particularly competitors).

Luckily for all of us, Mike Cohn of Mountain Goat Software and Kenny Rubin of Innolution have taken much of the pain away through the creation of the Comparative Agility[1] website. They explain that

> in Comparative Agility, we assume agile teams and organizations strive always to be better than their competition and their past selves. As such, there is no holy grail or "perfect ten" score to be achieved. In fact, there's no predefined best-in-class or "Agile Maturity Level 5" to be achieved. Rather, Comparative Agility assessments present the results of a set of survey responses in comparison to some other set of responses. For example, using Comparative Agility it is possible to compare a team, project or organization to:
>
> - The total set of collected responses;
> - Responses from organizations in the same industry;
> - Responses from similar types of projects (such as commercial software, websites, and so on); or
> - Responses from projects with similar lengths of experience at becoming agile.

The 75 questions of a Comparative Agility assessment are organized into seven dimensions and thirty-two characteristics. The seven dimensions represent

---

1. To take the Comparative Agility survey, go to http://comparativeagility.com.

broad classifications of changes to be expected of a team or organization as it becomes more agile. The seven dimensions are:

- Teamwork
- Requirements
- Planning
- Technical practices
- Quality
- Culture
- Knowledge creation

Each dimension is made up of three to six characteristics and a set of questions is asked to assess a team's score on each characteristic. (Cohn and Rubin 2010)

The survey is user friendly and offers some fascinating insight into relative progress.

I have confidence in tools such as the Comparative Agility assessment that are written and facilitated by genuine experts. However, I do have a warning for you: if comparing to others is the only benchmark you use, then in essence, you're letting others dictate your progress, and that can lead to stagnation. For example, if you take the survey and realize that you're doing particularly well in relation to other organizations, you may feel a false sense of security. First, your competitors might not have taken the survey. Second, and worse, you may feel that you are in the luxurious position of being able to enjoy your time at the top and take your foot off the continuous improvement pedal, and that is never a good idea.

Keep It Simple

If you really want to keep things simple, just ask three questions:

- Are your clients happier—are they remaining loyal and buying more products?
- Are your team members happier—are they abandoning ship or are they smiling more?
- Are your stakeholders happier—are they more relaxed and letting the team do its job rather than micromanaging?

In addition, the metric that should really interest you is the rate of Scrum adoption growth. Is Scrum delivering such great results that it is now beginning to spread across the broader organization, even crossing the chasm into other non-software related departments? For me, that is the ultimate success!

Spread the Good Word

In Australia, it is widely accepted that culturally, we're not very good at celebrating success—this trait, believe it or not, even has a label: "tall-poppy syndrome." Being humble and modest is at times admirable; however, when introducing change, celebrating success is critical to help maintain momentum, generate excitement, and encourage those who have been taking the risks. So, in this case, I say forget modesty and let the whole world know how well things are going! Conduct regular team meetings to discuss progress. Invite senior stakeholders to these sessions. Circulate emails, as discussed in Shortcut 25, with anecdotal stories to back up the statistics. Sing success from the rooftops! I don't care how you do it, but you should celebrate your continual improvement and let the team and the organization share in the glory.

Shortcut 29: Eyes on the Prize

In my formative years, I was obsessed with the game of football (or soccer to my fellow Aussies and friends in North America).

During lunchtime at school, a whole bunch of us would head down to the fields and play some extremely intense, pick-up games. We would rapidly organize into two teams, and then were off. When I look back at those enjoyable games, I am in awe at the amazing chemistry that seemed to automatically exist between us. Somehow, we all immediately worked out which position we would play in. Without the aid of uniforms, we were able to identify who was on each team simply by constantly talking. The dedication was outstanding (considering that nothing was at stake but daily pride), the interplay was amazing, and everyone seemed to know where everyone else was going to be. It was almost telepathic—if someone was caught out having to defend by himself, the rest of the team would sprint back to help out (even though they weren't necessarily defenders). But best of all was the tight camaraderie—winning or losing, everyone was always encouraging each other.

I was also fortunate to have had the opportunity to play soccer for my state at a national level. My expectations were so high for my first tournament because I would be playing with and against some of the best of the best in the entire country! We had slick uniforms, super-talented specialist players, an experienced manager with plenty of impressive plans up his sleeve, and significant individual motivation (the national team would be selected from this tournament). So, how did this tournament go? Did we perform like the stars we thought we were? The answer is an emphatic *no*—we were plagued by mediocrity! Why? What went wrong, you ask? Well, we squabbled and finger-pointed over every little mistake; our meticulous game plan failed as soon as someone got injured; we didn't know one another well, so we couldn't play to each others' strengths; driven by individual glory, teamwork was forgotten; and because of very rigid positional play, backup wasn't forthcoming when someone became outnumbered.

Bottom line was that this command-and-control approach to playing soccer (combined with a bunch of prima donnas) was much less effective than our self-organizing, lunchtime games.

How does this anecdote relate to our Scrum teams? Well, having read this far through the book, you will realize that there is a great deal of work to do as a Scrum-Master. Being inundated with so much to do, you may find it very difficult to keep your eye on the holy grail: the fostering of a truly self-organizing team, akin to our kick-ass lunchtime soccer teams.

Explaining Self-Organization

Let's now formalize (ironic choice of words, I know) what self-organization means, as it is often misinterpreted by the skeptics to mean something more akin to bedlam! I like Rubin's (2012) description:

> Self-organization is a bottom-up emergent property of a complex adaptive system. In such systems, many entities interact with each other in various ways, and these interactions are governed by simple, localized rules operating in a context of constant feedback. These types of systems exhibit interesting characteristics, such as being remarkably robust and producing amazing novelty.
>
> A development team has no top-down command-and-control authority that tells the team how to do its work. Instead, a cross-functionally diverse team of people organize themselves in the most appropriate way to get work done.

Self-organization is extremely powerful, as demonstrated by my soccer example, and this can be backed up time and time again just by observing nature. Watch an ant colony, a beehive, or a flock of birds, and you'll see clear applications of self-organizing behavior. Lyssa Adkins (2010) uses another great example from the world of entertainment when she describes her awe after watching a string quartet:

> These four guys sat down, and with no one looking at anyone, no one counting down, no one doing even as much as taking in a big breath, they just started to play . . . As they played, they managed the music themselves, shifting and correcting as the piece went on. No conductor needed.

Environments and Boundaries

Whenever you try to explain the benefits of self-organization to a skeptic, it is critical not to ignore references to boundaries. Skeptics who draw parallels between self-organizing teams and a group of headless chickens need to understand that responsible team members are the ones best equipped to determine how to do their work and when they think it will be done. A manager who likes to dictate these directions is simply not as qualified to make these calls in comparison to the team actually doing the work. By dictating these terms, all that the manager accomplishes is the provision of a false sense of control to the rest of the organization.

That being said, team members don't just magically wake up one morning in a state of fluent self-organization. Just like a plant, self-organization needs to be grown and nurtured in a particular environment with distinct boundaries, or it risks spreading wildly out of control and all over the neighbor's fence. These boundaries don't form themselves, nor do they stay maintenance-free. It is the ScrumMaster who needs to work closely with management to "Establish enough checkpoints to prevent instability, ambiguity, and tension from turning into chaos" (Takeuchi and Nonaka 1986).

These checkpoints or boundaries come in many shapes and forms (see Figure 10.2). Let's look at five of the big ones.

Scrum Rules

First, the Scrum rules. Even though there aren't any Scrum police who will jump out from behind the office coffee machine and fine you for not following the Scrum rules, a hefty fine might seem like a preferable option if the rules are not followed with discipline. If you've ever seen the bedlam that ensues when a soccer referee appears to get the rules wrong, you'll find a similar situation can erupt in a Scrum team if the rules become ambiguous or change frequently. By consistently enforcing and reinforcing the (small) set of Scrum rules, the team's conceptual self-organizing boundaries will be clearly established, allowing them to focus on actually doing the work.

FIGURE 10.2   Whether a soccer team or a Scrum team, self-organization leads to better results and more fun!

Team Makeup

The team members rarely get to determine who forms their ranks even though they are the ones that must work together to self-organize. Get the wrong mix of personalities and/or skill sets, and the lofty goal of self-organization goes out the window (see Shortcut 5). Even with the right mix of people, conflicts will occur and dynamics will change. The ScrumMaster should assist management in the selection of team members to ensure that the team has the natural predisposition to self-organize and work together as one.

Physical Environment

Shortcut 3 discusses the importance of the physical environment, and the reality is that unless you generate a physical working environment that enables the collocation of team members, self-organization is going to be more challenging (but definitely still doable). Creating a contained yet open space that is conducive to natural and regular verbal communication establishes the physical boundaries to allow the self-organizing team to easily connect without contrived, formalized communication channels.

Culture

If individuals are constantly on a mission to cover up their mistakes and point fingers at other people, then you can rest assured that the chances of attaining self-organizing status is somewhere between zero and nil. The ScrumMaster and management are responsible for providing a cultural safe haven for the team to feel relaxed about working together (see Shortcut 24). This culture needs to also foster a collective team desire to continuously seek improvement opportunities and try out new ideas without fear of failure.

Requirements

A fundamental tenet of Scrum is that the product owner (via the product backlog) determines what should be developed and in what order rather than it being up to the whim of the development team. In addition, the agreed-upon definition of done (see Shortcut 11) sets the clear quality boundary, ensuring that expectations between the product owner and development team remain aligned.

Ensuring that the developers understand the constraints inherent in the product backlog and definition of done is critical to allow them the freedom to self-organize and develop the requirements in the most optimal fashion.

The Infinite Role

It always bothers me when I hear noble exclamations similar to, "As great Scrum-Masters, we should always strive to make ourselves obsolete," referring to the fact that once the goal of team self-organization has been attained, the ScrumMaster becomes redundant. This is nonsense, and I'll tell you why.

First, change is inevitable. In the same way that a record-beating, all-star sporting team won't stay together forever, neither will a brilliant, self-organizing Scrum team. People move on, team members have off days, and companies undergo restructuring that causes teams to split up. Where there is the possibility for change, there is the requirement for a ScrumMaster.

Second, impediments are never predictable. No one knows what issues will pop up out of the blue that can't be resolved by the team, irrespective of how self-organizing they are. There are also impediments that shouldn't be tackled by the team, but by the ScrumMaster, to ensure maximum time is being spent on the actual development work.

Finally, perfection is impossible. Nothing in the world is perfect, and improvements can always be made, even to mature, self-organizing teams. Fine-tuning and helping teams make incremental improvements is much harder (but potentially more rewarding) than making the obvious fast-track improvements that are easily identified in less mature teams.

Shortcut 30: Shortcut to the Final Level

Yes, I know—you've heard it repeated ad nauseam that Scrum is "hard and disruptive" (Schwaber 2006), and I'm sure many of you will have learned this lesson firsthand.

I don't disagree with this contention, as Scrum certainly does come loaded with some serious transformational change stipulations. There are numerous hurdles to overcome, such as building cross-functional team cohesion; ensuring product owner empowerment; keeping high-performing, self-organizing teams together; and ensuring that senior stakeholders support the change from a systemic perspective.

However, I tend to look at Scrum in another way. I see it as completely infallible and always win-win. Sounds like a strange thing to say, doesn't it? Well, let me explain.

Looking in the Mirror

Remember in Shortcut 12 when I discussed that being able to constantly inspect and adapt the work being completed in a sprint is like the team looking frequently into a mirror to uncover small issues nice and early? Now, let's take that same principle to a macro level. Let's face it—your Scrum project might not work out. It might downright flop for a number of reasons. However, if you remain disciplined, follow the Scrum rules, and adhere to the key practices, then, at the very worst, Scrum will act like a mirror, helping you to uncover the dysfunctions that caused the project to fizzle. If you can identify these issues, you should consider it an accomplishment! It's just like physical health; if you're unwell, don't you want to know what is wrong with you so that you can choose a course of action to rectify the situation? Scrum is like a brilliant doctor with the ability to identify and diagnose all sorts of problems that you didn't even realize you had.

Choose Your Own Adventure

Please remember that Scrum is a light framework with only a few key rules and a limited set of practices. This book is certainly not trying to lay down the law on how Scrum should be implemented; it is simply offering a set of interpretations and opinions based on a specific set of experiences. Whether you choose to listen to my particular recommendations or not won't impact the fact that you are doing Scrum; so long as you stay within the bounds of the framework, you can truly choose your own adventure. Books like this one simply act as an optional travel guide for your journey. Just as for a vacation, all you really need is a passport, some money, and an understanding of the travel regulations and local laws, but apart from that, you are free to do what you like. Travel guides are not mandatory, but they can certainly help!

Experiment

In Shortcut 24, I offered some advice to help convince the conservative pessimists to free themselves from the fear of change. This advice is so powerful that it warrants being restated with additional gravity and emphasis in this final shortcut. If there are only three words that you remember from this entire book, they should be

TRANSPARENCY

INSPECTION

ADAPTATION

These three pillars of empirical process control form the foundation of Scrum and, if understood correctly, will ensure that you are always in a win-win situation. People don't like change for many reasons, and one of the core reasons is that they feel there will be no room to move once the decision to adopt something new has been made. But here's the thing: Scrum is open-minded. If something isn't working, there is a very simple guideline: inspect and adapt. By being open and transparent, you'll find it easy to inspect, and by regularly inspecting, you are able to adapt effectively. Adapting may include adjusting, reverting back to an old approach, or trying something totally new. A Scrum adoption should be seen as a big collection of small experiments (actions from your reviews and retrospectives) wrapped up in a big experiment (perhaps the Scrum pilot program that is initially run). If this is how Scrum is interpreted, there should never be any tears because at the end of the day, through transparency, inspection, and adaptation, the most appropriate happy path will eventually be identified to take your team and organization to the next level of efficiency. As Richard Buckminster Fuller (2008), a systems theorist, put it, "Every time a man makes a new experiment he always learns more. He cannot learn less."

Don't Rest on Your Laurels

Some of you might be at a stage where you are now feeling pretty happy; you've been instrumental in getting Scrum up and running, it's humming along nicely, and everyone is grinning from ear to ear. Time to sit back and let the good times roll, right? Wrong! Recall from Shortcut 4 that while you can certainly feel perfectly happy with the achievements made so far, you should never feel a sense of completion. Remember that nothing is perfect, so there will always be improvements to be made. Further, in a dynamic organization, nothing and no one stands still for long. Impediments can pop up at any time, team members will move on or get replaced, and departments could merge or split up. You should see your entire environment as one that is constantly in flux, irrespective of how placid it might seem at any specific point in time.

Flux requires a calm, guiding force that is able to react positively to change while smoothing out the creases in the team fabric before they become permanent wrinkles. With various staff coming and going at all levels, you need to be continuously educating the organization, and I'm not just talking about those involved in the software development efforts. Your ultimate goal is to convince every single person in your organization that "agility needs to be seen as a business strategy and not just something the IT guys do" (Kearns 2012). If agile becomes a part of the entire organization's DNA and culture, the cascade effect will make the implementation of Scrum software projects so much more natural.

Exceeding Expectations

It's funny, but when you immerse yourself in Scrum, you may uncover a fascinating side effect—it permeates into other areas of your life, becoming an innate way of thinking and behaving. For example, as I mentioned in Shortcut 11, I have used Scrum, with its associated artifacts and activities, at home to get our household chores done ever since our first baby came along. And I haven't stopped there. I have embraced the underlying ethos of Scrum in other day-to-day activities. How? I try to work (and play) at a consistent and sustainable pace; I focus more on completing a task, be it a chore at home or a job at work, in its entirety rather than trying in vain to juggle five things at once (an old habit of mine). I no longer need my 3-year life plans; instead I allow my future to take a more flexible and emergent course. Displays of dictatorial command and control behavior, whether in the workforce or household, make me wince now, when in the past I may well have been that dictating commander. Instead, I aim to always use persuasion principles (that I adopted as a ScrumMaster) more akin to the flowing, natural martial art of Aikido. In this sport, rather than using direct force, you subtly blend with your opponent and redirect his or her attention to where it should be focused. These days I'm always asking myself how I can get a positive response and reaction from others without having to revert to authority and unilateral commands. I also now run very regular introspective retrospectives on myself—usually during the solitary trip to work in the mornings rather than waiting for that short window of opportunity on the 31st of December to set all of my unrealistic and quickly forgotten New Year resolutions.

Final Wrap Up

When I set out on my Scrum journey, I was expecting it to change the way my teams worked for the better. I certainly didn't expect it to change many of my underlying philosophies and the way I behave in general. However, that is exactly what has happened. Not only has Scrum made me a better colleague and leader, but I truly believe it has also made me a better person.

My goal is to help extend Scrum's transformational qualities far outside the software environment, and I hope you are encouraged to join me.

Thank you for letting me share my thoughts with you, and I wish you a safe and enjoyable trip as you embark on the next leg of your exciting Scrum journey.

REFERENCES

Adkins, Lyssa. 2010. *Coaching Agile Teams: A Companion for ScrumMasters, Agile Coaches, and Project Managers in Transition.* Addison-Wesley.

Appelo, Jurgen. 2011. *Management 3.0: Leading Agile Developers, Developing Agile Leaders.* Addison-Wesley.

Beck, Kent. 1999. *Extreme Programming Explained: Embrace Change.* Addison-Wesley.

Beck, Kent, Mike Beedle, Arie van Bennekum, Alistair Cockburn, Ward Cunningham, Martin Fowler, James Grenning, Jim Highsmith, Andrew Hunt, Ron Jeffries, Jon Kern, Brian Marick, Robert C. Martin, Steve Mellor, Ken Schwaber, Jeff Sutherland, and Dave Thomas. 2001. *Manifesto for Agile Software Development.* www.agilemanifesto.org.

Benefield, Gabrielle. 2008. Rolling Out Agile in a Large Enterprise. In *Proceedings of the 41st Annual Hawaii International Conference on System Sciences.* IEEE Computer Society.

Bosworth, Andrew. 2009, November 20. Facebook Engineering Bootcamp. *Facebook Engineering's Notes.* www.facebook.com/note.php?note_id=177577963919.

Brooks, Frederick P. 1995. *The Mythical Man-Month: Essays on Software Engineering* (Anniversary Ed, 2nd Ed.). Addison-Wesley.

Carnegie, Dale. 1981. *How to Win Friends and Influence People* (Revised Ed.). Simon & Schuster.

Cohn, Mike. 2002. Alternative Scrum Release Burndown Chart. *Mountain Goat Software—Topics in Scrum.* www.mountaingoatsoftware.com/scrum/alt-releaseburndown/.

———. 2004. *User Stories Applied: For Agile Software Development.* Addison-Wesley.

———. 2007, April 12. Introduction to Scrum Methodology. A downloadable presentation from the Scrum Alliance website. http://scrumalliance.org/resources/47.

———. 2007, November. Why I Don't Use Story Points for Sprint Planning. *Succeeding with Agile: Mike Cohn's Blog.* www.mountaingoatsoftware.com/blog/why-i-dont-use-story-points-for-sprint-planning.

———. 2009. *Succeeding with Agile: Software Development Using Scrum.* Addison-Wesley.

————. 2011, November 28. In Defense of Large Numbers. *Succeeding with Agile: Mike Cohn's Blog.* www.mountaingoatsoftware.com/blog/in-defense-of-large-numbers.

————. 2012, January. Recommendations Not Rules. *Succeeding with Agile: Mike Cohn's Blog.* www.mountaingoatsoftware.com/blog/recommendations-not-rules.

Cohn, Mike and Kenny Rubin. 2010. What is Comparative Agility? *Comparative Agility.* www.comparativeagility.com/overview.

Conway, Melvin. 1968. Why Do Committees Invent? *Datamation* 14(4):28–31.

Crispin, Lisa and Janet Gregory. 2009. *Agile Testing: A Practical Guide for Testers and Agile Teams.* Addison-Wesley.

Deemer, Pete. 2011. *Manager 2.0: The Role of the Manager in Scrum.* Available from www.goodagile.com/resources/roleofthemanager10.pdf.

Deemer, Pete, and Gabrielle Benefield, Craig Larman, Bas Vodde. 2010. *The Scrum Primer, Version 2.0.* www.scrumprimer.com.

DeMarco, Tom and Timothy Lister. 1999. *Peopleware: Productive Projects and Teams,* 2nd Ed. Dorset House.

Derby, Esther and Diana Larsen. 2006. *Agile Retrospectives: Making Good Teams Great.* Pragmatic Bookshelf.

Dwyer, Mike. 2010. Scrum is a silver WHAT and you want to put it WHERE? *Big Visible–Agile Coaching Blog.* www.bigvisible.com/2010/07/scrum-is-a-silver-what-and-you-want-to-put-it-where/.

Fowler, Martin. 2006, May 1. Continuous Integration. From Martin Fowler's website. http://martinfowler.com/articles/continuousIntegration.html.

Fowler, Geoffrey A, and Scott Morrison. 2010, October 31. eBay Attempts to Clean Up the Clutter. *Wall Street Journal.*

Fuller, Richard Buckminster. 2008. *Operating Manual for Spaceship Earth.* Ed. Jaime Snyder. Lars Müller Publishers.

Goddard, Paul. 2011. ScrumMaster: Role or Job? Session presented at Scrum Alliance Global Gathering: London 2011.

Greenleaf, Robert K. 2008. *The Servant as Leader.* Greenleaf Center for Servant Leadership.

Grenning, James. 2009, February 6. Planning Poker Party (the Companion Games). James Grenning's Blog. www.renaissancesoftware.net/blog/archives/36.

Humble, Jez. 2010, August 13. Continuous Delivery vs Continuous Deployment. *Continuous Delivery Blog.* http://continuousdelivery.com/2010/08/continuous-delivery-vs-continuous-deployment/.

Jeffries, Ron. 2010, December 24. Which End of the Horse? *XProgramming.com: An Agile Software Development Resource.* http://xprogramming.com/articles/which-end-of-the-horse/.

Jenkins, Nick. 2008. *A Software Testing Primer. An Introduction to Software Testing.* www.nickjenkins.net/prose/testingPrimer.pdf.

Jobs at Google. 2005, July 28. Zurich office photos. Images available at https://picasaweb.google.com/photos.jobs/ZurichOfficePhotos.

Kearns, Martin. 2012. *Agile and Portfolio/Program Management.* Session presented at Agile Australia 2012, Melbourne.

Keith, Clinton. 2010. *Agile Game Development with Scrum.* Addison-Wesley.

Kniberg, Henrik. 2011. *Lean from the Trenches: Managing Large-Scale Projects with Kanban.* Pragmatic Bookshelf.

Maher, Rob. 2011. *Increasing Team Productivity: A Project Focus Creates Waste and Leaves Value on the Table.* Scrum.org Whitepaper retrieved from the Scrum.org website. www.scrum.org/Portals/0/Documents/Community%20Work/Increasing%20Team%20Productivity.pdf.

Mar, Kane. 2012. Scrum 101—Scrum and Extreme Programming (XP). YouTube.com. July 13. www.youtube.com/watch?v=Pav4YxhsQbc.

Moses, Asher. 2012, May 18. Brain Drain: Why Young Entrepreneurs Leave Home. *Sydney Morning Herald.*

Owsinski, Bobby. 2009. *The Studio Musician's Handbook (Music Pro Guides).* Hal Leonard

Parkinson, C. Northcote. 1993. *Parkinson's Law.* Buccaneer Books.

Pichler, Roman. 2010. *Agile Product Management with Scrum: Creating Products That Customers Love.* Addison-Wesley.

Pink, Dan H. 2011. *Drive: The Surprising Truth about What Motivates Us.* Riverhead Trade.

Poppendieck, Mary and Tom Poppendieck. 2009. *Leading Lean Software Development: Results Are Not the Point.* Addison-Wesley.

Rubin, Kenneth S. 2012. *Essential Scrum: A Practical Guide to the Most Popular Agile Process.* Addison-Wesley Professional.

Schwaber, Ken. 2004. *Agile Project Management with Scrum* (Microsoft Professional). Microsoft Press.

———. 2006. *Scrum Is Hard and Disruptive.* Available from www.controlchaos.com/storage/scrum-articles/Scrum%20Is%20Hard%20and%20Disruptive.pdf.

———. 2011, April 7. Scrum Fails? *Ken Schwaber's Blog: Telling It Like It Is.* http://kenschwaber.wordpress.com/2011/04/07/scrum-fails/.

Schwaber, Ken, and Jeff Sutherland. 2011. *The Scrum Guide.* Downloadable at www.scrum.org.

Schwartz, Tony. 2012, January 23. Why Appreciation Matters So Much. *Harvard Business Review.* http://blogs.hbr.org/schwartz/2012/01/why-appreciation-matters-so-mu.html.

Scrum Alliance. 2012. *Core Scrum.* Available from http://agileatlas.org/atlas/scrum.

Senor, Dan, and Saul Singer. 2009. *Start-up Nation: The Story of Israel's Economic Miracle.* Grand Central Publishing.

Shore, James, and Shane Warden. 2007. *The Art of Agile Development.* O'Reilly Media.

Silverman, Rachel Emma. 2012, February 2. No More Angling for the Best Seat; More Meetings Are Stand-Up Jobs. *Wall Street Journal.*

Spolsky, Joel. 2007. *Smart and Gets Things Done.* Apress.

Takeuchi, Hirotaka, and Ikujiro Nonaka. 1986, January. The New New Product Development Game. *Harvard Business Review.*

Wilson, Woodrow. 1916, July 10. Address to the Salesmanship Congress. Detroit, Michigan.

Wojcicki, Susan. 2011. The Eight Pillars of Innovation. *Think Quarterly: The Innovation Issue—July 2011.* Available from www.thinkwithgoogle.com/quarterly/innovation/8-pillars-of-innovation.html.

Yip, Jason. 2011, August 29. It's Not Just Standing Up: Patterns for Daily Standup Meetings. From Martin Fowler's website. http://martinfowler.com/articles/itsNotJustStandingUp.htm.

INDEX